D0382067

WALLS

AND

WELCOME

MATS

IMMIGRATION
AND THE
AMERICAN DREAM

LARS ORTIZ

TWENTY-FIRST CENTURY BOOKS / MINNEAPOLIS

In loving memory of my mom, Talia.
Thank you for welcoming me into your Dream.

Twenty-First Century Books™
An imprint of Lerner Publishing Group, Inc.
241 First Avenue North
Minneapolis, MN 55401 USA

For reading levels and more information, look up this title at www.lernerbooks.com.

Main body text set in Adobe Garamond Pro.
Typeface provided by Adobe Systems.

Library of Congress Cataloging-in-Publication Data

Names: Ortiz, Lars, 1984– author.
Title: Walls and welcome mats : immigration and the American dream / Lars Krogstad Ortiz.
Description: Minneapolis : Twenty-First Century Books, [2023] | Includes bibliographical references and index. | Audience: Ages 13–18 | Audience: Grades 10–12 | Summary: "From hope for a better future to the backlash of xenophobia and nationalism, this book examines the history and current issues surrounding immigration in America"— Provided by publisher.
Identifiers: LCCN 2022006745 (print) | LCCN 2022006746 (ebook) | ISBN 9781728423999 (library binding) | ISBN 9781728445427 (ebook)
Subjects: LCSH: Emigration and immigration—Juvenile literature. | Immigrants—United States—Juvenile literature. | United States—Emigration and immigration—Juvenile literature.
Classification: LCC JV6035 .O78 2023 (print) | LCC JV6035 (ebook) | DDC 304.8— dc23/eng/20220325

LC record available at https://lccn.loc.gov/2022006745
LC ebook record available at https://lccn.loc.gov/2022006746

Manufactured in the United States of America
1-49222-49348-9/6/2022

TABLE OF CONTENTS

INTRODUCTION

Migration, moving from one place to another, is common among humans and other animals. Through the study of early fossil records and modern genetic testing, scientists know that humans, or *Homo sapiens*, first lived in Africa about two hundred thousand years ago.

Scientists think that humans migrated to other parts of the globe around sixty-five thousand years ago. Some moved east, crossing Asia. Between fifteen thousand and twenty thousand years ago, or perhaps earlier, some ventured across what used to be a land bridge between modern-day Russia and Alaska. They probably traveled on foot or near the shoreline in boats. They continued to travel across North and South America and are likely the ancestors of Indigenous Americans.

The first Europeans in North America were Vikings, or seafarers from Scandinavia. More than one thousand years ago, they reached the lands that have now become Canada. In the 1500s, Spanish and French explorers came to North America in search of valuable natural resources, with a desire to colonize the land. Many British explorers and colonists followed. Around twenty million Indigenous people lived in North America at the time.

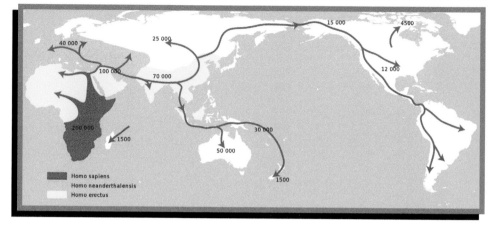

For many years, scientists and historians theorized that humans first reached the Americas via a land bridge that disappeared under the ocean long ago. This Bering Land Bridge would have been between modern-day Siberia and Alaska. That theory has been questioned recently due to new archeological discoveries and an acknowledgment of the oral histories of Indigenous Americans. A new theory has been proposed that humans sailed along the shores of the Pacific Ocean, subsisting on abundant kelp forests along the way.

British colonists declared their independence from Great Britain in 1776 and formed the United States. The new nation was already a diverse one, with Indigenous peoples and immigrants from all over Europe calling this land their home. The United States quickly grew. By the mid-1800s, it was an economic powerhouse that attracted people from all over the globe. Immigrants from far and wide came to this "New World" for many reasons: to seek new opportunities, to escape religious or ethnic persecution, or to start a new life. They planted roots and contributed their own customs, languages, and cultures to the fabric of American society, helping create one of the most culturally diverse countries in the world.

However, some citizens resented the influx of immigrants. As immigration to the United States increased, so did the backlash against immigrants. From individual acts of violence and threats to official government actions, such as the Chinese Exclusion Act of 1882, many US immigrants have had to endure unwelcoming treatment from other Americans.

In 1863, construction began on the first transcontinental railroad built in the United States. Historians estimate that fifteen thousand Chinese migrants helped build the railroad's western half.

Why are some Americans unwelcoming to new immigrants? Some fear people who are different. They see unfamiliar people as strange or scary, as an "other." Some people fear that immigrants will take their jobs. Others blame immigrants for society's problems. Divisive words by politicians can increase a dislike or fear of people from other countries.

Some natural-born citizens—people born in the United States—claim that immigrants are a drain on US resources and economy. This is untrue. Immigrants contribute greatly to the economy and the culture of the United States. Over the centuries, immigrants have built railways and highways; dug canals; and worked in mills, mines, and factories. Immigrants have always been the backbone of the US economy. From science and technology to the arts and politics,

In 2019, immigration rights activists protested in front of the US Supreme Court as it heard arguments for ending the Deferred Action for Childhood Arrivals (DACA) program.

immigrants and the children of immigrants have proven to be some of the most ambitious and creative people in the country.

Almost every American has an immigration story to tell, whether they moved here yesterday or their ancestors arrived hundreds or even thousands of years ago. As we explore the history of immigration, think about your story. When did your journey begin? Why did your family move to where you live? When they arrived, did they encounter walls trying to stop them or welcome mats making them feel at home? If you don't already know the answers to these questions, it might be worth investigating your roots and ancestry by making a family tree, researching old photos and documents, interviewing relatives, or taking a DNA test.

What is your immigration story?

CHAPTER 1

AMERICAN STORY

To understand the story of immigration in the United States, we need to understand how it started. In 1606, King James I of England allowed the Virginia Company of London to colonize the territory of Virginia. This for-profit company sent 104 men to settle in an area called Jamestown. In the early seventeenth century, a group seeking religious liberty from the Church of England formed a colony in Plymouth, Massachusetts. Over time, other colonies were settled in Maryland and the Carolinas.

From the moment Europeans arrived in North America, they encountered a population of Indigenous peoples with rich histories and cultures. While many Europeans traded with Indigenous peoples, they also desired their lands. Wars broke out between colonists and eastern tribes, leading to many deaths on all sides. In addition, Europeans brought diseases to which Indigenous people had no natural immunity. One of the most deadly, smallpox, killed millions of Indigenous people. The terrible result of these land-grabbing wars and death from disease was that many Indigenous peoples were pushed out of their homelands. Unable to hunt freely or grow crops, many even died of starvation. Others were killed in warfare with the European settlers.

English king James I granted land in North America to the Virginia Company of London in the charter of 1606. But the land was already home to several Indigenous Algonquian tribes. The English not only fought them for the land, but also kidnapped many Algonquians and even forcibly converted some to Christianity.

REVOLUTION

As more and more immigrants came to North America, the number of English colonies expanded to thirteen. As the colonies grew, so did their discontent with the monarchy in England. The British Empire wanted to grow, and America's vast land and natural resources were a part of that plan, but the colonists wanted to expand their own fortunes and opportunities. They wanted to freely grow their own businesses and determine their own destinies, and they increasingly viewed themselves as distinctly American, not citizens of the British Empire. Decisions that impacted their lives were being made across the ocean by a disconnected king who had little regard for the colonists' quality of life.

THE TRUE STORY OF THE FIRST THANKSGIVING

The Wampanoag inhabited portions of modern-day Massachusetts and Rhode Island for more than ten thousand years before Europeans arrived on the continent. They had their own established communities, beliefs, and governments when the Plymouth colonists arrived in the fall of 1621. Although the two groups spoke different languages and came from vastly different cultures, the Wampanoag saw that the colonists were starving and taught them to grow corn, squash, and other crops. The colonists had a three-day harvest feast, and in celebration they fired muskets. Wampanoag warriors feared an invasion and rushed to the scene. They laid down their arms after seeing the celebratory nature of the occasion and joined the festival. The peace between the English colonists and the Wampanoag did not last. Colonists went on to steal Indigenous land, and in the 1670s, the two groups went to war.

The last straw came after England went to war with France. To recoup the high cost of war, England imposed direct taxes on the American colonies for the first time. The taxes were an economic hardship, and the colonists didn't want to pay them if they had no representatives in the English Parliament in London. The phrase "No taxation without representation" became a popular rallying cry for these new Americans.

In 1773, Americans staged a protest that would become known as the Boston Tea Party. To protest a tax on tea, a group tossed the British East India Company's cargo of tea into the Boston Harbor. England responded by closing the port and sending in troops. The Americans began to arm themselves. After British forces confiscated the colonists' growing supply of weapons in Lexington and Concord, Massachusetts,

the colonies formed the Continental army under George Washington to counter the British threat. The American Revolution (1775–1783) began. Washington was initially unhappy with the quality of his new army, as it was neither professional nor particularly well trained. Instead, it was composed of farmers, blacksmiths, and all manner of colonists who were able-bodied.

Most American colonists did not have independence in mind when war broke out—they simply wanted their rights to self-determination respected. But when an attempt at brokering peace failed, a gathering of representatives from each colony descended on Philadelphia. Called the Continental Congress, this group decided their only remedy was to proclaim independence from Britain. The Declaration of Independence, written mainly by Thomas Jefferson, was adopted on July 4, 1776. This date became known as Independence Day. The signing of this document was a bold move that sent shock waves across the Atlantic Ocean and the world.

This engraving depicts the British retreat from Concord in April 1775. British troops were given secret orders to search for military supplies from colonial militias and destroy them. The colonists learned about the secret attack ahead of time and were able to force the British troops into a tactical withdrawal.

The Declaration of Independence laid out principles that would help guide the nation for centuries to come. Chief among them was that all people should be treated the same way and that all have fundamental rights. The document also said that all government power should come from the people. Its preamble, or opening, reads:

> WHEN in the Course of human Events, it becomes necessary for one People to dissolve the Political Bands which have connected them with another, and to assume among the Powers of the Earth, the separate and equal Station to which the Laws of Nature and of Nature's God entitle them, a decent Respect to the Opinions of Mankind requires that they should declare the causes which impel them to the Separation.
>
> We hold these Truths to be self-evident, that all Men are created equal, that they are endowed by their Creator with certain unalienable Rights, that among these are Life, Liberty, and the Pursuit of Happiness.

An Irish immigrant and Philadelphia business owner named John Dunlap spread the word by printing copies of the Declaration of Independence. In those days, printing documents was not as easy as pressing a button. It required a whole room full of equipment. Each individual letter had to be placed on a plate before ink was applied to the type. Then paper was pressed between two plates to transfer the ink. This time-intensive process kept Dunlap up all night, and he printed the first two hundred copies of the radical document by candlelight. Dunlap, both immigrant and patriot, went on to fight in George Washington's army as an officer during the American Revolution. After eight long years of battle, Britain withdrew, and the United States of America was formed.

The United States Constitution was initially drafted in 1787, but it was argued over extensively before it was ratified in 1788 by a majority of states. The Constitution replaced the earlier Articles of Confederation, which had outlined the first laws of the United States during the American Revolution.

The US Constitution, the founding document of the country, was ratified by the Congress of the Confederation in 1788. The next year, the new US Congress submitted twelve constitutional amendments to the state legislatures for approval. Ten of these were ratified by the states and passed into law. They are known as the Bill of Rights.

AMERICAN DREAMS AND NIGHTMARES

Not everyone was free or enjoyed rights as new US citizens. Only landowning men were allowed to vote in the new United States. Indigenous people continued to be pushed off their lands. Black Americans had severely restricted civil and political rights. Americans with European backgrounds continued to enslave the vast majority of Black Americans and to purposely limit the rights of free Blacks. On August 20, 1619, the first slave ship arrived to the American colonies. It was a Dutch ship with a cargo of human beings captured from Spanish slave ships they had intercepted. The captive Africans were quickly enslaved and were regularly bought, sold, and traded. They were forced to work and follow the commands of their enslavers. The slave trade continued, and by 1750, about 240,000 enslaved Africans lived in the

In the 1860s, photographer Henry P. Moore captured images of life for former enslaved people in the American South. During the Civil War, many plantation owners abandoned Union-occupied lands. This meant many people were no longer enslaved, yet were not considered legally free until the Emancipation Proclamation of 1863. Many formerly enslaved people joined the Union to fight in the Civil War, such as these sailors on the USS *Vermont*.

HAMILTON: MAN AND MUSICAL

One of the most influential framers of the US Constitution, Alexander Hamilton, was born in Nevis, a British island in the Caribbean Sea. He was a proponent of a strong centralized federal government, and his writing in *The Federalist Papers* still influences political and legal thinking. He became the nation's first secretary of the treasury. His colorful life was eventually turned into the immensely popular musical *Hamilton* by Lin-Manuel Miranda.

British colonies. After the English, they were the largest demographic group. By the time the United States became a nation, the number of enslaved people had doubled.

A NEW WORLD

A French immigrant who settled in New York, J. Hector St. John de Crèvecœur wrote *Letters from an American Farmer* in 1782. In this book, he described his optimistic view of American diversity:

> What then is the American, this new man? He is either European, or the descendant of a European, hence that strange mixture of blood, which you will find in no other country. I could point out to you a family whose grandfather was an Englishman, whose wife was Dutch, whose son married a French woman, and whose present four sons now have four wives of different nations. He is an American, who leaving behind him all his ancient prejudices and manners, receives new ones from the new mode of life he has embraced, the new government he obeys, and the new rank he holds.

He continued, "Here individuals of all races are melted into a new race of man, whose labors and posterity will one day cause great changes in the world." His observation would prove to have staying power. Soon people from every corner of the globe would begin to pour into the nation.

In the 1770s, when the United States declared its independence as a country, it was home to mainly British colonists and enslaved Black people. A small number of Spanish, French, Dutch, and German settlers lived in the colonies and the territories. Soon more immigrants came—many more.

The new US government promoted exploration and settlement west of the Mississippi River after the Louisiana Purchase, a land deal with France in 1803. For $15 million, the United States purchased French territory, doubling the nation in size.

As the nation expanded, Native Americans were pushed farther west. The US government played an active role in this process. For example, in 1830 President Andrew Jackson signed the Indian Removal Act. This act forced Indigenous peoples from their ancestral lands in the American South. Most were sent to reservations. Those who did not go willingly or who fought back were killed. The expansion gave the US government the larger territory it desired, but countless Indigenous lives were uprooted or lost. In the following decades, similar forced expulsions took place all across the American West.

THE TRAIL OF TEARS

The Indian Removal Act forced the Native nations in the southeastern United States, east of the Mississippi River, to move westward. Tens of thousands of Indigenous Americans walked more than 5,000 miles

(8,047 km) to land promised to them by the government. The forced migration was long and dangerous. The Native people were at times made to walk in chains and at gunpoint. Disease spread and thousands of people died. Their forced march came to be known as the Trail of Tears.

Elizabeth "Betsy" Brown Stephens was a Cherokee woman who walked the Trail of Tears in 1838. Over twelve thousand Cherokees were displaced and forcibly moved west of the Mississippi.

COAST TO COAST

The population of the United States grew from five million in 1800 to more than twenty-three million in 1850. This rapid expansion created a desire for more land and opportunities. In 1845, Americans spoke of Manifest Destiny, the idea that God wanted Americans to occupy all the land from North America's east coast to its west coast.

On May 20, 1862, President Abraham Lincoln signed the Homestead Act to encourage people to move into the western part of the country. The act gave settlers 160 acres (65 ha) of federal land if they settled and farmed the land for five years. The Homestead Act attracted many new immigrants from Europe, as well as citizens from the East Coast.

American Progress is a painting by artist John Gast. Painted in 1872, it depicts an allegory of American westward expansion and the idea of Manifest Destiny. The woman is called Columbia and is a common symbol of the United States in that era. Here, Columbia is shown bringing light and infrastructure to the west. Art like *American Progress* perpetuated the idea that white Americans brought civilization to a dark and wild western territory, justifying the seizure of land from Indigenous peoples.

The act also gave more than 9 million acres (3.6 million ha) of land to railroad companies. These companies needed workers, and they advertised for them overseas. This brought even more immigrants to the United States.

Back in Europe, "America letters," letters written by immigrants, were passed from person to person and published in local papers. These letters assured the people back home that the United States had such plentiful food and farmland that "produces so richly without fertilizer that [your homeland] can no more be compared to America than a desert to a garden of herbs in blossom."

But these dreams of bountiful food and fertile land were not so easily fulfilled. European immigrants first had to cross a vast ocean to reach America's shores. These journeys were long and perilous. Many people embarked on the journey with only the belongings they could carry, including clothing and the food they would need for the trip. On board ship, many endured crowding, seasickness, lice, and bedbugs. The infestations and overcrowded conditions invited disease. Many of these "coffin ships" arrived on America's shores with significantly fewer people than when they left. Despite all this hardship, the lure of a new life in a new land brought millions to America's shores.

MANAGING ARRIVALS

At first, the federal government left the management of arriving immigrants to the states. New York, the East Coast's epicenter of arriving immigrants, got organized early. In 1855, the state decided to process its immigrant arrivals at Castle Garden, an old fortress in Manhattan. Eight million immigrants passed through Castle Garden before it was closed in 1892.

New York's next immigration processing center was Ellis Island. From 1892 to 1924, twelve million people passed through its doors. As they approached the island, they saw the Statue of Liberty in New

THE GOLDEN DOOR

The Statue of Liberty has become a symbol of hope, freedom, and democracy to the whole world. Originally a gift from France, it stands on an island in New York Harbor, where it has welcomed millions of immigrants and visitors since its dedication in 1886. Engraved on a bronze plaque inside the statue are the words of poet Emma Lazarus:

> Give me your tired, your poor,
> Your huddled masses yearning to breathe free,
> The wretched refuse of your teeming shore.
> Send these, the homeless, tempest-tost to me,
> I lift my lamp beside the golden door!

The Statue of Liberty was funded jointly by France and the United States. The US funded the construction of the pedestal. Construction of the statue was completed in France by 1884. The disassembled statue arrived in New York the next year.

York Harbor. Many viewed the site with awe and hope. This was the beginning of their journey in a new land. They went on to start new lives, cultivate new farms, start new businesses, and contribute to society.

On the West Coast, Angel Island in San Francisco Bay served as the nation's Pacific coast immigrant center from 1910 to 1940. Here, immigrants from Asia began their shot at living the American dream.

CHAPTER 2

OUT OF MANY, ONE

The United States' motto since its founding has been *e pluribus unum*. This Latin phrase means "out of many, one," and it is found on the nation's official seal and all its money. This is because the United States is formed out of many peoples and also out of many states and territories..

Immigrants to the United States come from nearly every country in the world, making it among the most diverse nations in the world. Mexicans represent the largest share of US immigrants with numbers of more than 11 million, or about 25 percent of all immigrants. The next most populous group is from China, with 2.7 million immigrants (6 percent) and then from India, with 2.4 million (6 percent). People from the Philippines make up 4 percent of all US immigrants, and those from El Salvador round out the top five with 3 percent. By region of birth, Asian immigrants comprise 28 percent of the total immigrant population; Europe and Canada, 13 percent; the Caribbean, 10 percent; Central America, 8 percent; South America, 7 percent; the Middle East and North Africa, 4 percent; and sub-Saharan Africa, 5 percent.

The rest of this chapter breaks down the US immigrant experience by country of origin or ethnic/religious group. It gives just a snapshot of each group and its main motivations for emigrating. The countries

IMMIGRANT VS. EMIGRANT VS. MIGRANT

What's the difference? It all depends on the direction. All three words come from *migrare*, the Latin verb that means "to move from one direction to another." People are considered emigrants when they leave their country—they have emigrated from somewhere. They might say, "My ancestors emigrated from Norway." Someone is an immigrant when they have arrived at their destination. They might say, "My mom immigrated to America. She is an immigrant from Mexico."

An easier way to remember the difference is that *immigrant* begins with the letter *i*, as in going *into* a country, and *emigrant* begins with *e*, or *exiting* a country. Meanwhile, a migrant is a person who travels anywhere, whether to another country or within the borders of a country.

these people came from have long histories, and while at certain period in time significant numbers of people found reason to leave, these moments don't represent the full scope of life in these places.

GERMANY

In 1848, Germany was in political upheaval. The German Confederation was a loose coalition of independent states. Those Germans who sought unification into a single country were failing, and the political divisions caused widespread rebellion and fighting. Many chose to leave Germany at this time. Large populations of German immigrants settled on the East Coast in New York and Pennsylvania. Others went to Missouri, Illinois, Minnesota, Wisconsin, and Texas. Like many immigrants, they faced hostility and criticism, but despite this, German Americans persevered and prospered. By 1860, 1.5 million people of German descent had settled in the United States. By 1900, 5 million called the nation their new home, and those numbers continued to grow.

In 1874, German emigrants boarded a steamer in Hamburg, Germany setting out for the United States. Around 1.5 million Germans settled in the United States in the following decade, the greatest influx of German immigrants in US history.

IRELAND

Ireland was the most densely populated country in Europe in the early 1800s. Most of the land was controlled by English landowners, who rented farms to the Irish at high rates. Many Irish farmers grew potatoes. Enough of the crop could be grown on a small plot of land to feed a family, while the rest of land was used to grow food for their English landlords. By the 1840s, roughly half the population of Ireland was surviving on potatoes. When a fungus called potato blight arrived in 1845, the effects were devastating. The crop turned to black mush and became inedible. Starvation and disease were rampant. After six years of famine, almost one million Irish people had died.

To escape their plight, many Irish came to America. By 1870, 4.7 million Irish immigrants had settled on the East Coast, mostly in New York and Boston. Life in the United States was better than it was in

Mary G. Harris, known as Mother Jones, was an Irish-born American teacher who worked around the United States to organize unions. In 1903, she helped organize a children's march to protest the use of child labor in mines and factories.

Ireland, but like the Germans, they faced discrimination from natural-born Americans. Hard manual labor jobs were often the only employment they could find. Many worked in unsafe factories, while others built roads or railroads.

SCANDINAVIA

It is believed that Scandinavian Vikings were the first Europeans to reach North America, but immigrants from Scandinavia (Norway, Sweden, Denmark, Finland, and Iceland) did not arrive in large numbers until the 1850s. In Norway and Sweden, which were then politically unified, farming opportunities were already limited due to the mountainous terrain, cold climate, and short growing season. In the previous century, the area's population had doubled, which reduced the availability of viable farmland and led to occasional famines.

More than one million Scandinavians, the majority Norwegians, came to America between the early 1800s and 1924. They settled in cities, such as Chicago and New York, but most made their way to the upper Midwest: Minnesota, Wisconsin, and the Dakotas. Scandinavians dreamed of land ownership and fertile farms, and the cold climate in these states was similar in many ways to their homelands. They quickly established themselves in the region. In the twenty-first century, more Minnesotans claim Scandinavian ancestry than people in any other state.

There are statues of Leif Eriksson throughout the United States commemorating the influence of Scandinavians on American history and culture. They can be found everywhere from Boston, MA, to Chicago, IL, to Saint Paul, MN.

POLAND

Poland's geographic location in Europe, with Germany to the west and Russia to the east, has put it in the center of many conflicts throughout history. From 1795 to 1919, three neighboring powers controlled Poland. Poland achieved independence in 1919. After World War II (1939–1945), it fell under partial control of the Soviet Union (a group of republics that included Russia), until its fall in the early 1990s. With so much historical turmoil in their homeland, Polish immigrants have come to seek political freedom and a better standard of living in the United States.

Between 1880 and 1914 about two million Poles came to the United States. They established themselves in major cities, such as Chicago, New York, and Detroit, as well as in rural areas, such as western Pennsylvania. Coal mining was prevalent in Pennsylvania, and since many of these immigrants had similar jobs in Poland's Carpathian Mountains, the area was a natural fit.

ITALY

The movement for Italian independence and unification, called the Risorgimento, put Italy under one flag in the mid-1800s, but it also

led to massive inequality. Much of Italy, especially the south, suffered from disease, malnutrition, and poverty. Between 1880 and 1924, more than four million Italians immigrated to the United States. Their primary destination was New York City, where eventually an enclave of immigrants called Little Italy became a place of communal support. But many Italians settled as far west as California. By the 1920s, Italian Americans were about 10 percent of the nation's population. Although they faced stiff opposition and were painted with discriminatory stereotypes, they became an important part of American society and are the nation's fifth-largest ethnic group.

Little Italy began on Mulberry Street in New York City, but it swiftly expanded into surrounding streets as more immigrants arrived. The neighborhood shrank in the 1930s as many Italian Americans moved out of the city. In 2010, the neighborhood was listed as a historic district by the National Register of Historic Places.

CHINA

Increased territory and new systems that helped increase crops led to several population booms in China. By 1850, the population grew to over 400 million people. Partly due to the growing population and partly due to the damage of the Opium Wars at the hands of the British and French Empires, social, economic, and political unrest was growing in China. Many left their homeland for more social and economic power.

Very few Chinese immigrants lived in America then. With the discovery of gold in California in 1848, a gold rush began. People from inside the United States and abroad came to the West Coast hoping to strike it rich. This scramble for fortune brought the first substantial influx of Chinese immigrants, about twenty-five thousand in the three years after the gold rush began. They came to find *gam saan*, or "gold mountain." While some did find what they were looking for, most found low-paying cooking and cleaning jobs in the mining towns or found jobs building railroads.

By 1870, there were about sixty thousand Chinese immigrants in the country, most of them in California. As Chinese immigrants continued entering the US, they increasingly faced ugly discrimination and racism from other Americans, embodied by the passage of the Chinese Exclusion Act of 1882. This legislation effectively banned Chinese immigrants from entering the country. The law was struck down in 1943 after the United States and China became allies in World War II. After more reforms in the 1960s, more than 350,000 Chinese came to the United States in the 1970s and 1980s. Despite hardships and discrimination, Chinese Americans created enclaves called Chinatowns in many major cities. These neighborhoods established a sense of community and safety amid a sometimes hostile and discriminatory environment.

JAPAN

When almost four hundred thousand Japanese immigrants made their way to Hawaii starting in the 1880s, Hawaii was still an independent

country. The United States annexed the island in 1898. By then, Hawaiians of Japanese ancestry were the majority population. Much of the island's Japanese population worked tough manual labor jobs, especially in the sugarcane industry. Japanese immigration to mainland America swelled after Hawaii's annexation, from both the newly American Hawaiian islands and also Japan itself. Most Japanese Americans settled on the West Coast and worked at agriculture jobs. Many eventually bought their own farmland. The issei, Japanese-born immigrants, and nisei, their children who were born in America, would go on to thrive in their new home. By 1924, around one hundred thousand Japanese lived on the mainland.

Although they faced harsh racism and discrimination, it would pale in comparison to what Japanese Americans endured during World War II. The United States fought against Japan during this war, which led many European Americans to falsely suspect Japanese Americans of disloyalty to the United States. Consequently, the government forced Japanese Americans to live in concentration

In 1942, the United States government forced Japanese Americans and their families to pack their belongings and relocate to internment camps. Nearly two thirds of the occupants of these camps were US citizens.

camps during World War II. In modern times, Japanese Americans are the third-largest immigrant community of Asian descent in the United States. The majority live in California, Hawaii, Oregon, and Washington.

THE PHILIPPINES

The Philippines, comprising over seven thousand islands, was a Spanish colony from 1521 until 1898. After the Spanish-American War, the islands became America's first major overseas territory. From the Philippines, many people started to move to Hawaii. By

REFUGEES

People leave their homelands for various reasons. Refugees are people who flee their country of origin due to fear of danger or persecution for a variety of reasons, which can include race, religion, nationality, or political opinion. When they cross another country's border, they can apply for asylum, a legal status that allows people to stay in the country because they may be in danger in the country they have left. If the country they enter approves their application, they are then allowed to stay. Each country sets its own immigration laws, and certain nations accept more refugees than others. Sometimes, when there is mass migration because of war, natural disaster, or economic crisis, nations place refugees in temporary camps. Are refugees considered immigrants? Legally speaking, no. Refugees are forced to leave their lands of origin due to violence or another crisis, while immigrants choose to leave.

Another type of refugees, climate refugees, are likely to become more common in the near future. Earth is warming because of a buildup of carbon dioxide in the atmosphere, which comes from people burning massive amounts of coal, oil, and natural gas. As Earth has warmed, storms have increased in intensity, droughts and wildfires have increased, glaciers have melted, and coastal areas have flooded. All these factors are causing people to flee their homes and settle elsewhere.

1930 there were around 100,000 Filipinos living in Hawaii. After the passage of the Tydings-McDuffie Act, the Philippines won its independence in 1946. As slow economic growth and several corrupt presidencies stretched over decades, Filipinos immigrated to the United States in droves. By 2000, more than 1.4 million had immigrated to the US. Nursing became a profession of choice for many of these immigrants. Filipinos are the second-largest Asian American and Pacific Islander group in the nation, and almost half live in California. Many also live in Hawaii, New York, New Jersey, and Illinois.

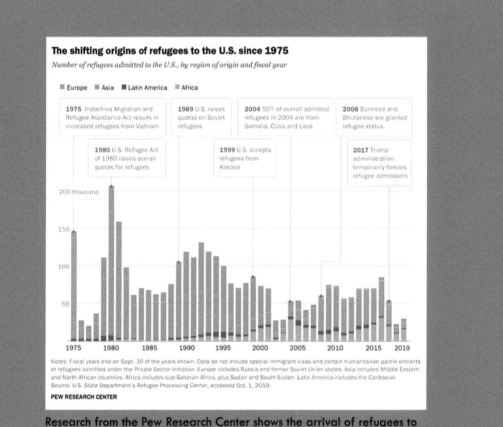

Research from the Pew Research Center shows the arrival of refugees to the United States reached a peak after President Jimmy Carter signed the US Refugee Act.

KOREA

After decades of influence from countries like China, the US, and Japan, Korea became a Japanese colony from 1910 to 1945. After World War II, it was divided into North Korea, backed by China and Russia, and South Korea, backed by the United States. The Korean War (1950–1953) between these two nations left millions dead. Afterward, the North became an isolated authoritarian nation, and the South gradually embraced democracy. South Korea eventually became an economic powerhouse, while North Koreans are detached from the rest of the world under the leadership of one tyrannical family.

Immigration from South Korea to the United States began after the war as people tried to find work and escape political unrest. American families adopted around one hundred thousand postwar orphans, and some American servicemen married Korean women who accompanied their husbands back to the United States. A wave of immigration began in the 1960s after work permits were granted to Korean doctors and nurses, and the wave continued as immigration restrictions were eased in 1968. By 1980, 350,000 Koreans had settled in the United States. By 2000, the nation was home to more than 1.1 million Korean Americans, and those numbers still grow. A third of the Korean American population lives in Southern California, while the rest are spread nationwide, particularly in New York and New Jersey.

VIETNAM, LAOS, AND CAMBODIA

People have lived in Vietnam for at least 20,000 years. But it was divided in the 1950s after decades of resisting French invasion. In 1964 the United States sent troops to assist the South in its struggle against the North, whose leaders embraced a political philosophy called communism that the US opposed. This was the long and bloody Vietnam War (1954–1975). America's direct military action in Vietnam lasted until 1973. The neighboring nations of Laos and Cambodia also fell under communist rule, and thousands would make their way to the

United States as refugees. After 1975, 1.1 million Vietnamese refugees left their homeland. The United States was their primary destination, although others settled in Australia, Canada, and the nations of Europe. By the late 1970s, 14,000 refugees a month were authorized to enter the United States, and by the mid-1980s, about 500,000 resided there. Half settled in California or Texas. In the twenty-first century, more than 2 million Vietnamese Americans live in the United States.

PROFILE: **HALIMA ADEN**

Halima Aden was born in a refugee camp in Kenya in 1997 after her parents fled a war in Somalia. After moving to Minnesota, she became a finalist in the Miss Minnesota USA pageant, signed with a fashion modeling agency, and soon was walking runways in New York City and Milan, Italy. She became the first woman to appear on the cover of an American fashion magazine wearing a hijab, a headscarf worn by many Islamic women. In 2021, she was interviewed as one of the BBC's 100 Women about why she left the modeling industry.

SOMALIA

Somalia is located in northeastern Africa bordered by Ethiopia, Djibouti, the Gulf of Aden, and the Indian Ocean. Researchers believe people have lived there for about 7,000 years. Italy and Britain colonized areas of Somalia in the late nineteenth century after years of declining Turkish rule. After the nation gained independence from Italy and Britain in 1960, a dictator emerged to rule there from 1969 to 1991. When he was overthrown in a coup, the capital city Mogadishu was thrown into chaos as different groups battled for power and control. A humanitarian crisis ensued, with almost 400,000 Somalis dying of starvation as a result of the fighting. Over a decade, about 1 million refugees escaped Somalia. Many fled to neighboring countries. By 1999, 30,000 were given asylum in the United States. In the twenty-first century, more than 150,000 Somalis live in the United States, with their biggest populations in Minnesota and Maine.

Representative Ilhan Omar is the first Somali American to serve in the United States Congress. Born in Mogadishu in 1982, Omar became a naturalized citizen in 2000.

CUBA

The Indigenous Ciboney, Guanahatabey, and Taíno peoples occupied Cuba until Spanish colonization in the fifteenth century. Cuba gained independence again after the Spanish American War of 1898. From 1933 to 1959, Cuba struggled under Fulgencio Batista, whose rule included widespread corruption and poverty. Fidel Castro replaced him during the Cuban Revolution in the 1950s. Castro was popular with many Cubans in part because he brought a higher standard of living to the country. But when he started executing and arresting those who opposed him, many Cuban refugees came to the United States. They traveled to Florida, which sits less than 100 miles (161 km) from Cuba. About two hundred thousand came in the initial wave. By 2000, that number had risen to six hundred thousand. In the twenty-first century, about two million Cubans reside in the United States. More than half are Cuban-born. The majority live in and around South Florida, with the biggest population in Miami.

PROFILE: **CELIA CRUZ**

Celia Cruz, the "Queen of Salsa," was born in 1925. Cruz inspired audiences around the world to get up and dance. She was born in Havana, Cuba, and performed there from an early age. She found widespread success in the United States in the 1970s, including winning two Grammy Awards. Cruz also appeared in many movies and telenovelas. Cruz became the face of salsa music for generations.

HAITI

Located in the Caribbean Sea, Haiti is largely occupied by Black Latin Americans. It was the first nation to abolish slavery after declaring itself free from French rule in 1804. But it faced many political and economic hardships after, including influence from countries like the US. A brutal father-son dictatorship gained power for three decades after a devastating 1954 hurricane. When their rule ended in 1986, economic and political chaos ensued. With poverty rampant, many Haitian immigrants found a new home nearby in the United States. In 2010, a devastating earthquake killed hundreds of thousands and displaced more than 1.5 million Haitian people. Haitian immigration tripled from 1990 to 2018 and rose 17 percent after the earthquake. In 2021, after another large earthquake and political instability caused by the assassination of the island nation's president, more Haitian refugees entered the United States. More than 60 percent of Haitian immigrants and refugees live in vibrant communities in Florida and New York. Altogether, more than 700,000 Haitians live in the United States. They make up the fourth-largest Caribbean immigrant group in the United States after Cubans, Dominicans, and Jamaicans.

PUERTO RICO

A Caribbean island inhabited by the Taíno people at the time of European arrival, Puerto Rico was a colony of Spain until the end of the Spanish-American War in 1898. It became a US territory and later became the Commonwealth of Puerto Rico. In 1917 from 1493, all Puerto Ricans were granted US citizenship. Therefore those who live in the United States are not technically immigrants. Many call them internal migrants—those who move within the borders of their own country. When living permanently in the United States, Puerto Ricans have all the rights of citizens, including the right to vote. However, Puerto Ricans residing on the island of Puerto Rico cannot vote in US elections.

Puerto Rico has a distinct identity, language (Spanish), and culture, so, like many other immigrants, some Puerto Ricans experience discrimination in the United States. In the twenty-first century, more than five million Puerto Ricans live on the US mainland, surpassing even the population of the island. They are the second-largest Hispanic group in the United States.

MEXICO

Although the United States is home to significant numbers of immigrants from all of Latin America, the vast majority are from Mexico, on the southern US border. Before Spanish colonization, Mexico was home largely to Indigenous groups like the Mayan and Toltec peoples. Mexico won independence from Spain in 1821. At the time, Mexico controlled the territories of Texas, California, New Mexico, and most of Arizona, Nevada, Utah, and Colorado. After the United States annexed Texas in 1845, the Mexican-American War ensued. With the Treaty of Guadalupe Hidalgo in 1848, North American territories previously claimed by Mexico became part of the

THE BRACERO PROGRAM AND CIRCULAR MIGRATION

The Bracero program, also known as the United States Emergency Farm Labor Program, was created in 1942. This guest worker policy allowed millions of Mexican men to enter the United States temporarily and work at agricultural jobs. Employers were supposed to hire them only if they could not find Americans to fill the jobs, and employers were required to provide housing and transport the workers back to Mexico when their contracts were done. However, Mexican laborers in this program were often not given adequate housing or paid what was promised. Many workers suffered, and the program ended in 1964. This type of migration, where people come and go based on the availability of work, is known as circular migration.

United States. A section of the Rio Grande became the new international border, and the one hundred thousand Mexicans who chose to stay in their homes north of this line became US citizens. As their descendants say, "We didn't cross the border. The border crossed us."

In the 1910s, revolution and civil war consumed Mexico, and

THE AMERICAN DREAM

"American Dream" is possibly one of the most successful marketing slogans of all time. Millions of people—both inside and outside the United States—strive for it.

Although it is unknown when the phrase was first used, one of the first examples comes from the *Chicago Tribune* in 1916. A February 7 article read, "If the American idea, the American hope, the American dream . . . are not worth fighting for to maintain and protect, they were not worth fighting for to establish."

In his 1917 novel *Susan Lenox: Her Fall and Rise*, David Graham Phillips wrote that "fashion and home magazines" have prepared people "for the possible rise of fortune" that "is the universal American dream and hope."

Historian James Truslow Adams used the term most prominently in his book *The Epic of America* (1931). In the preface, he writes of that "American dream of a better, richer, and happier life for all our citizens of every rank which is the greatest contribution we have as yet made to the thought and welfare of the world. That dream or hope has been present from the start. Ever since we became an independent nation."

The phrase has become so common that it is often considered cliché, but its ability to quickly capture the nation's ideals and spirit is precisely the reason it continues to have so much power. A survey of citizens by the American Enterprise Institute and the National Opinion Research Center at the University of Chicago found that of those surveyed, 85 percent believed that having "freedom of choice in how to live" was essential to the American dream. In the same survey, over the next two decades, this unrest caused more than five hundred thousand Mexicans to look for better conditions north of the border. During the Great Depression of the 1930s, with jobs in short supply, many Mexicans were deported (expelled from the United States) to reserve jobs for European Americans.

83 percent expressed that "a good family life" was key, 16 percent believed becoming "wealthy" was essential, and only 45 percent indicated that having a "better quality of life than your parents" was crucial. Just 49 percent of respondents said that "having a successful career" was necessary. This shows that while income and workplace success are still important, many people have come to view the American dream as being less about money and upward mobility and more about having a strong community, a healthy family, and a good quality of life.

THE LADDER OF FORTUNE.

Industry and Morality bring solid rewards.   Idle schemes and speculations yield poverty and ruin.

The Ladder of Fortune is a lithograph produced by Currier and Ives in 1875. It presents an allegory for the virtues that many Americans believed would lead to success. This view of the American Dream did not take into account the history of slavery and oppression that kept many people in poverty.

As the American economy boomed later in the twentieth century, so did the need for labor. Many of those who came from Mexico to work in the United States did so without legal authorization from the US government. After a severe economic crisis in Mexico in the 1980s, large numbers of Mexicans sought a more stable life by traveling north. During that decade, the US Border Patrol turned back about one million immigrants a year at the southern border, while more than sixty thousand Mexicans entered the country legally every year. Many settled in California and other parts of the American Southwest, but Mexican immigrants have made their homes in every state. Numbering fourteen million, Americans of Mexican descent are the largest immigrant population in the country, and they are an integral part of the US economy and society.

ETHNICITIES AND RELIGIONS

Not all immigrant groups come from a single country of origin. Some trace their origins and identities to an ethnicity or religion that exists across borders in many nations.

HMONG

The Hmong are an ethnic minority who trace their roots back thousands of years to the mountains of Southwest China. Under persecution, they migrated south and established vibrant communities in Laos, Thailand, Myanmar, and Vietnam. They preserved their distinctive language, customs, and traditions in their adopted homelands. During the Vietnam War, the United States recruited the Hmong as allies in its fight against communism. After the war ended, Hmong refugees were granted asylum in America. Between 1976 and 1990, about one hundred thousand Hmong settled in the United States. In the twenty-first century, close to four hundred thousand Hmong Americans live in the United States, with the largest enclaves being in Minnesota and Wisconsin.

JEWS

The Jewish people, most of whom practice the religion of Judaism, are an ethnic group with roots dating back thousands of years. Originally from lands that became Israel in the Middle East, the Jews migrated over many centuries, with large numbers settling in Eastern Europe. Because of persecution there, millions chose to emigrate in the late 1900s. Between 1880 and the 1910s, almost 2.5 million Jewish immigrants arrived in the United States.

During World War II, the German government systematically killed six million European Jews, an event known as the Holocaust. Those who could fled Europe. At the time, restrictive US immigration laws, created in the 1920s, were still being enforced. So from the late 1930s to the late 1940s, only about 170,000 Jews were admitted to the United States, with thousands more turned away despite an outcry for safe asylum. In the twenty-first century, more than 7 million Jewish Americans reside in the United States—a greater population than even in the Jewish homeland of Israel.

Haym Salomon was a Polish-born Jewish American who assisted the Continental Army during the American Revolution. After being captured by British forces, Salomon worked as an interpreter for German soldiers on the side of the British. During this time, he helped prisoners of war escape and encouraged German soldiers to desert. When his actions were discovered, he escaped to Philadelphia to continue assisting the Continental Army.

MUSLIMS

Muslims—people who practice the religion of Islam—account for one-quarter of the world's population. The first large group of Muslims came to America against their will. They were enslaved Africans who had practiced Islam in their home countries before being taken by slave traders. Historians estimate that up to 20 percent of enslaved West Africans in the American colonies were Muslim, although they were not allowed to practice their faith in America.

In the 1870s, a wave of Muslims from the Middle East came to the United States, mainly from Syria and Lebanon. By the early 1900s, New York had a flourishing Muslim community. When US immigration laws relaxed in the 1960s, Muslims from Egypt and other

The United States has been a country of many religions from the beginning. Islam was first brought to the Americas by enslaved people in the 1600s, though many enslaved people were forced to convert to Christianity.

PROFILE: **NIKOLA TESLA**

Nikola Tesla was born in Croatia in 1856. He came to the United States in 1891 to pursue his scientific dream "to harness the forces of nature to the service of mankind." He succeeded and is credited

with inventions that transformed the world, including innovations that led to radio, X-rays, and wireless computer technology. He also invented a motor that runs on alternating current, technology that powers many modern machines.

Middle Eastern nations arrived, as well as some from Yugoslavia and Albania who were seeking religious freedom. In 1979, after the Iranian Revolution, more than 100,000 Iranian Muslims came to the United States. In the twenty-first century, more than 3.5 million Muslims call the United States home.

CHAPTER 3

BACKLASH: PART I

Immigrants who come to the United States usually face a difficult transition to a new life. From finding a place to live to finding a way to support themselves financially to making friends and finding their way around, the life of an immigrant is not easy. Every country regulates immigration at its borders to make it easier or harder for immigrants to enter the country and live there. The US government creates laws and policies that shape US immigration.

It is not just laws that can make life difficult for immigrants. Once in the United States, immigrants are often met with resistance from people who already live here. This resistance may include hurled insults, a glare at the supermarket, or a neighborhood being unwelcoming. Sometimes the motivation is racism or xenophobia. Some natural-born Americans believe that the religious practices of certain immigrants are bad or inferior to their own beliefs. Sometimes this discrimination can turn into hate crimes, which are crimes—often violent—motivated by the victim's race, sexual orientation or identity, or membership in a certain group.

Negative attitudes toward immigrants can also arise from resentment and a fear that immigrants are taking jobs that "belong" to other citizens or that they're using government services and living

in a country that doesn't "belong" to them. Those feelings are not new. Anti-immigrant views have been around since America's early colonial days. Perhaps it is human nature to be suspicious of what is new and different. Psychologists have studied this fear, and some think that the fear of people or things that are new or different is deeply rooted in our brains. Others believe it is a learned behavior taught by parents, schools, and society. Still others believe it is a mix of both. No matter where this fear comes from, it is important to recognize and understand it.

AMERICA WELCOMES YOU

The United States is known for its ideal of freedom, but freedom for whom? The framers of the Constitution, or founders, are often glorified. They were brilliant and ambitious. They thought deeply about democracy and government. They were people of action and determination who risked their lives to create a new country. But they were also complicated and flawed human beings.

Many of the founders owned enslaved people, and some had negative views on immigrants, even though many of them, such as Alexander Hamilton, were immigrants themselves. George Washington, who became the first US president, gave conflicting messages on immigration. As the head of the Continental Army, Washington had many immigrants in his ranks. After the American Revolution, he declared, "The bosom of America is open . . . to the oppressed and persecuted of all Nations and Religions." This bold invitation was acted upon by millions. But he also privately wrote, "I have no intention to invite immigrants, even if there are no restrictive [government] acts against it. I am opposed to it altogether." In 1794, during his presidency, Washington wrote about immigration to John Adams, the second president of the United States. He said, "Except of useful mechanics and some particular. . . . men and professions, there is no use of encouragement [of immigrants]."

Immigrants didn't just serve in the Continental Army. Some also commanded troops. Marie-Joseph Paul Yves Roch Gilbert du Motier, Marquis de La Fayette, was a French aristocrat who traveled to the United States to fight in the American Revolution at the age of 19. He fought and commanded American forces in many battles before returning to France to seek French support for the American cause.

Many early Americans were open to accepting immigrants they viewed as useful but rejected those they considered undesirable. Statesman Benjamin Franklin noticed the large numbers of Germans moving to Pennsylvania in 1751 and deemed them to be undesirable. He wrote, "Why should the [German] Boors be suffered to swarm into our Settlements, and by herding together establish their Language and Manners to the Exclusion of ours? Why should Pennsylvania, founded by the English, become a Colony of Aliens [foreigners], who will shortly be so numerous as to Germanize us instead of our Anglifying them, and will never adopt our Language or Customs."

Gaining US citizenship was a desire of many early immigrants. Being a citizen not only made it easier to find work but also made it easier to travel in and out of the country. Perhaps most powerfully, citizenship granted a person a greater say in deciding the rules and policies that governed their daily lives through the right to vote, though this privilege was only granted to white men at the time.

Congress addressed the issue of citizenship when it passed the Naturalization Act of 1790. Naturalization refers to the process of becoming a citizen of a country. The law put limits on who could be naturalized: only "any Alien being a free white person . . . of good character," who had resided in the country for two years. That was later changed to five years, but non-whites were still excluded until 1870, when Congress passed a law including "aliens of African nativity" or "African descent" to be naturalized. Indigenous Americans—whose ancestors had lived in the Americans for thousands of years—were not granted citizenship until the Indian Citizenship Act of 1924. And it wasn't until 1952 that immigrants from all Asian countries were given naturalization rights.

The citizenship of children born in the United States to immigrants was not fully addressed until 1868 with the passage of the Fourteenth Amendment to the Constitution. It stated that any person born in the United States was considered a citizen, regardless of where their parents were born. This is known as birthright citizenship, and it was opposed by many extreme anti-immigrant groups at the time.

BUT NOT YOU

The first major immigration legislation passed by Congress was the Immigration Act of 1882. With the passage of this law, the federal government signaled to states that it was taking control of immigration policy. The act restricted immigration for criminals, the insane, and anyone "unable to take care of him or herself." It also set a "head tax" of fifty cents per person to the cover costs of processing and screening the enormous influx of immigrants at that time.

That year another piece of immigration legislation came to define the growing anti-immigrant movement. During the gold rush and construction of the Central Pacific Railroad, businesses readily hired Chinese immigrants in the western states. At the height of the Central Pacific Railroad's construction, which lasted for most of the 1860s,

80 percent of the workers were Chinese men. The railroad believed they worked harder and were more dependable than other immigrants and American citizens. They also tended to work for less pay.

Due to racist attitudes and resentment of Chinese employment, anti-Chinese hostility was rampant, and this discrimination eventually became law. The Chinese Exclusion Act of 1882 banned all Chinese workers from entering the country and forbade Chinese immigrants from becoming citizens. The law was supposed to last ten years, but it was first renewed and then enacted permanently. Only in 1943 was this legal act of discrimination repealed. The act severely reduced Chinese immigration, but it had exemptions for immediate family members of Chinese already in the United States as well as for students, teachers, diplomats, merchants, and other limited categories of Chinese persons.

The US government first put patrols on the nation's southern and northern borders with Mexico and Canada not to keep out Mexicans or Canadians, but to keep out Chinese. They were held on cramped ships for weeks and sometimes years while authorities determined if they qualified for the act's exemptions. With diseases, starvation, and violence increasing on the detention ships, in 1910 the government opened Angel Island in San Francisco Bay. It became known as the Ellis Island of the West.

With cheap Chinese labor difficult to come by after the Chinese Exclusion Act, many businesses on the West Coast turned to Japanese workers. Japanese immigrants came to the United States to escape poverty and sometimes to avoid the high taxes that the Japanese government imposed on its residents to fund its modernization and industrialization efforts. Many came directly from Japan, but many others came from Hawaii, where hundreds of thousands of Japanese were already living. When they arrived, they faced the same resistance and hostility that the Chinese had faced. In 1901, California's governor called Japanese immigrants a "menace," saying that they posed as great a threat as the "peril from Chinese labor."

In 1907, the informal Gentlemen's Agreement was enacted to halt Japanese workers from coming to America. It was agreed to by President Theodore Roosevelt and the Japanese government, which not only wanted to slow the flow of emigrants leaving Japan but also wanted to avoid a harsh law similar to the Chinese Exclusion Act. The agreement led the Japanese government to deny passports to workers who wanted to enter the United States, and the US government agreed to deny entry to Japanese immigrants who attempted to enter with passports issued by other countries. As with the Chinese Exclusion Act, the agreement had exceptions. Immigrants already in the country could bring over their wives and children. Some women agreed to marry men they didn't know just to get to the United States. They were called picture brides because a matchmaker would pair immigrant workers with potential brides using just photographs.

The Gentlemen's Agreement didn't stop the hostility Japanese immigrants were facing. Like many immigrant groups, the Japanese opened small businesses, but their businesses were routinely vandalized. Smashed windows were common in some neighborhoods as were rotten eggs and fruit thrown at shops and employees. The anti-Japanese hysteria peaked in 1913, when California passed a state law that banned foreigners or "aliens ineligible for citizenship" from owning farms or holding long-term leases. The Alien Land Law did not specifically mention Asians, but it was specifically designed to discourage their immigration and make the lives of these immigrants as difficult as possible. Because the law discriminated against all immigrants not allowed to naturalize, it also affected Chinese, Korean, and Indian immigrants.

While Asian immigrants on the West Coast faced discrimination, xenophobia, and racism, the mostly European immigrants arriving in the East Coast during the 1800s also faced hostility. Those who were not of English descent faced discrimination based on race, culture, and country of origin. More than 60 percent of immigrants between 1830 and 1860 were from Germany and Ireland, and to many people the influx of German and Irish immigrants was undesirable.

Germans settled in most major US cities—especially Philadelphia, Chicago, New York, and New Orleans, where they faced much discrimination. They spoke German or English with a German accent, making them easy to identify as outsiders. Some natural-born Americans did not like their custom of using Sundays for outings and recreational sports instead of church. Others objected to their apparent fondness for beer. Most simply did not like that they were foreign.

The Irish faced fiercer hostility than most of the Germans because almost all Irish immigrants were Roman Catholic. Among the Protestant American majority, Catholicism was viewed with suspicion and hostility because the head of the Catholic Church, the pope, had great influence over Catholics. Some believed the pope, who lives in the Vatican in Italy, would try to take over the United States. They also believed that Catholics in America would put the pope's beliefs ahead of their belief in democracy and that their loyalty to the Catholic Church would outweigh their loyalty to the country. (Over one hundred years later, President John F. Kennedy faced similar fears over his Catholic faith.) American inventor Samuel Morse remarked in 1835 that he was seeing an "increase of Roman Catholic cathedrals,

All four of President John F. Kennedy's grandparents were children of Irish immigrants to the United States.

churches, colleges, convents . . . in every part of the country; in the sudden increase of Catholic emigration; in the increased clannishness of the Roman Catholics, and the boldness with which their leaders are experimenting on the character of the American people."

As starvation due to the potato famine in Ireland worsened, more and more Irish immigrants came to the United States. The majority of them settled in Boston and New York City. When Irish Catholics opened private Catholic schools that were separate from the public school system, some natural-born Americans saw this as evidence of their resistance to assimilating, or blending in with the larger US society.

Other groups also faced opposition. When a large wave of Italian immigration began in the 1880s, these immigrants were greeted with discrimination based on their predominantly Catholic faith and also their dark coloring. Employers denied them jobs, and many natural-born Americans shunned them. In 1912, a US congressional committee debated whether Italians could be considered "full-blooded Caucasians [white people]." Some called Italians "biologically and culturally less intelligent" than other Americans.

NATIVISTS AND KNOW NOTHINGS

A nativist movement grew in response to the rapid increase in immigration in the mid-1800s. Nativists believe that people born in their country are more important than people born in other countries. American nativism took many forms. Organizations formed to oppose the immigration of specific groups of people, such as the American Protective Association, an anti-Catholic group that opposed Irish immigration. Anti-immigrant political parties were formed. The Nativist Party in New York published a newspaper called the *Spirit of Seventy-Six*, which promoted anti-immigrant views.

The nativist political movement expanded in 1855 to a national party, called the American Party, popularly called the Know Nothing

Party. It started as a secret society of Protestant Anglo-Saxons, who when asked about their membership in the group would respond, "I know nothing." During the party's height, it included more than one hundred members of Congress, eight governors, the majority of six state legislatures (including California and Massachusetts), and thousands of local politicians. They wanted to deport all immigrant "beggars" and criminals, make Bible readings required in all public schools, remove all Catholics from public office, and increase the naturalization period from five to twenty-one years.

Christopher Phillips, a professor of history at the University of Cincinnati in Ohio, says the Know Nothing movement shares three traits with all other nativist movements throughout history. The first trait is an adoption of nationalism. Nationalism is a devotion to a country above all else, usually at the expense of other people and countries. The second trait is religious discrimination. The Know Nothings discriminated against Catholics. Third, nativist movements combine an appeal to working-class people with an appeal to upper-class politicians. Although the Know Nothing Party lasted only a few years, its legacy has never died in the United States, where nativists still rail against immigrants.

MORE RESTRICTIONS

Between 1890 and 1920, immigration to the United States was at its peak. The immigrant ancestry of more than one hundred million Americans can be traced to the wave of arrivals from this era. With immigration in full swing, especially from eastern and southern Europe, and with anti-immigrant sentiments growing, Congress passed a series of laws that severely restricted access to America's shores.

In 1921, the Emergency Quota Act was passed. It added two elements to immigration law that still apply: numerical limits and a quota system to formulate those limits. The act limited the number of immigrants from any country to 3 percent of the foreign-born people of that nationality living in the United States as of the 1910 census. This meant that people from western Europe were much more likely to be admitted than those from anywhere else, since people of western European heritage already made up the bulk of the national population. The law did not apply to "white-collar" immigrants, or those with professional jobs, and due to lobbying by the business community, which wanted workers from south of the border, who often were willing to work for lower wages than other Americans, the law also did not apply to immigrants from Latin America.

The Immigration Act of 1924, also known as the Johnson-Reed Act, restricted immigration even more drastically. It replaced all previous laws about Asian immigration and essentially banned it. It also set a new quota of 165,000 total immigrants per year for countries of the Eastern Hemisphere (all of Europe, Asia, Africa, Australia, and the Pacific Islands). Quotas for individual countries were lowered to 2 percent of their existing representation in the US population, and those numbers were based on the 1890 census instead of the 1910 census, which the previous immigration laws had used. The quotas imposed by this law severely reduced immigration from Italy, Greece, and Poland, as well as the immigration of eastern European Jews. This law also denied

UNITED STATES CENSUS

The census is a population count of all those living in the country. It is required by the Constitution and takes place every ten years. The census includes all citizens, noncitizen legal residents, noncitizen long-term visitors, and undocumented immigrants. The census does not just let the government know who lives where. It is also used to allocate congressional spending and to set each state's number of representatives in the House of Representatives. For historians studying immigration, the census provides especially valuable data, with numbers dating back to the first census in 1790.

admittance to homosexuals and those with mental or physical disabilities. It funded deportations and the creation of the US Border Patrol.

With immigration from most countries limited, anti-immigrant sentiments then turned to undocumented immigration (sometimes called illegal or unauthorized immigration). The Undesirable Aliens Act of 1929, known as Blease's Law, criminalized border crossings outside of official ports of entry. This law was primarily passed to restrict Latin American immigration, especially immigration from Mexico.

Although the immigration laws of the 1920s had a great impact on immigration in the United States, the Great Depression, beginning in 1929, had an even bigger effect. With the global economy in freefall from this worldwide financial collapse, jobs became scarce and international travel became rare. Only 500,000 immigrants entered the United States during the 1930s—a massive decline from the previous twenty years, when more than 12 million immigrants arrived. The onset of World War II further extended the immigration standstill. During the war, immigration was mostly restricted to 120,000 spouses and children of American soldiers who had married overseas, as well as 416,000 postwar European refugees.

In 1952, with the Cold War (1945–1991) in full swing, anti-communist sentiment was on the rise. Congress passed the Immigration and Nationality Act, also called the McCarran-Walter Act. It restricted immigration from eastern European countries suspected of having communist ties or sympathies. The act said that immigrants also needed to have "good moral character," which meant they could not be alcohol or drug abusers, illegal gamblers, or polygamists (people who are married to more than one spouse simultaneously).

Despite all the restrictions in the new law, it slightly increased immigration from China and Japan for the first time in decades and gave preference to immigrants with advanced degrees, technical skills, and other traits considered desirable. In the 1950s, 2.5 million immigrants came to the United States.

JAPANESE INTERNMENT

In the aftermath of Japan's bombing of Pearl Harbor in Hawaii on December 7, 1941, which pulled the United States into World War II, an anti-Japanese frenzy led President Franklin Roosevelt to sign an order that relocated more than 120,000 Japanese Americans to concentration camps. Of those incarcerated, more than 60 percent were US citizens. Forced to leave their homes, businesses, and farms, they lived behind barbed wire for two years in crudely built barracks guarded by the military. They were released after the war to try to rebuild their lives, but for many, the damage lasted a lifetime. Japanese American internment is considered one of the worst civil rights violations committed by the US government, and in 1988 the government issued a formal apology, along with $20,000 in payment to each internee who was still alive then.

Many Japanese Americans had fought for the United States in World War I. Despite their previous service, many of these veterans were sent to concentration camps such as the Santa Anita Assembly Center.

COMMUNISM

In the 1800s, German philosophers Karl Marx and Friedrich Engels developed the political and economic theory of communism. It called on working-class people to seize power from the wealthy, such as factory owners and landlords. In communist theory, private property is abolished and resources are distributed equally among all people. In practice, communist governments have not lived up to their promise of equality. They have mainly operated as totalitarian states, with nearly complete power over the lives of citizens. During the Cold War, the United States and the Soviet Union fought for global supremacy, with each power backing their ideals of capitalism or communism respectively.

As the civil rights movement of the 1960s highlighted racial inequalities in the United States, lawmakers took a new look at immigration policies. Past laws, especially of the 1920s, sought racist objectives, such as preserving "the ideal of US homogeneity," which meant that everyone in the United States should look and act the same. To counteract this, the Immigration and Nationality Act of 1965, or Hart-Celler Act, repealed quotas based on nationality. This allowed increased immigration from previously restricted places such as eastern and southern Europe, Asia, Africa, and the Middle East. A new annual limit of 290,000 immigrants was set, with 170,000 from the Eastern Hemisphere and 120,000 from the Western Hemisphere. A new quota system gave priority to relatives and children of US citizens, professionals, people with technical skills, and refugees.

The last major laws affecting immigration in the United States were passed in 1996. The Personal Responsibility and Work Opportunity Reconciliation Act mostly dealt with federal, state, and local benefits, such as welfare and food stamps. The law stipulated that

President Lyndon B. Johnson signed the Immigration and Nationality Act of 1965 on Liberty Island on October 3, 1965. Regarding the system this law was replacing, Johnson said, "This system violated the basic principle of American democracy . . . It has been un-American in the highest sense, because it has been untrue to the faith that brought thousands to these shores even before we were a country."

legal immigrants could not receive federal benefits for the first five years in the United States and that undocumented immigrants were ineligible to receive any benefits.

The Illegal Immigration Reform and Immigrant Responsibility Act set legal immigration at 675,000 people annually and allowed up to 100,000 refugees to enter the country per year. The law also attempted to decrease undocumented immigration by cutting down on circular migration, increasing border enforcement, and punishing those in the United States who were undocumented. But the law was difficult to enforce, and undocumented immigration, particularly from Latin America, continued to increase.

CHAPTER 4

IMMIGRATION IN THE TWENTY-FIRST CENTURY

More than one million immigrants arrive in the United States every year. According to the Pew Research Center, a nonpartisan think tank, between forty-four and forty-five million individuals who live in the United States were born in another country. Foreign-born individuals make up about 13.7 percent of the total US population, significantly higher than 1970's 4.7 percent, a few years after the major immigration reform laws of 1965. (The record remains at 14.8 percent, set in 1890 during the last great waves of historical immigration.) The United States is home to more immigrants than any other country in the world.

FINDING A HOME

Immigrants live in every state in the nation, but most (more than 60 percent) live in western and southern states. The states with the highest immigrant populations are California with 24 percent, Texas with 11 percent, and Florida with 10 percent. Most immigrants live in twenty major metropolitan areas. New York City, Los Angeles, and Miami have the largest shares.

Why do immigrants concentrate in certain areas of the country? Although reasons vary, this phenomenon is partly due to a desire to

PROFILE: ADRIANA OCAMPO

Adriana Ocampo dreamed of space exploration as she looked up at the stars from her rooftop in Buenos Aires, Argentina. After her family

moved to the United States, she studied engineering and planetary geology and took a job with the National Aeronautics and Space Administration. Her research led to the discovery of the Chicxulub crater in Mexico, the site of the asteroid impact theorized to have killed most life on Earth, including the dinosaurs, about 66 million years ago. She has also worked on missions to study Mars, Jupiter, and other planets.

live near other immigrants from their home countries or to live close to family members. The other major reason is employment. Agriculture and technology jobs, two industries in which many immigrants work, tend to be concentrated in certain regions.

LEGAL VS. ILLEGAL IMMIGRATION

Journalists and politicians often make a distinction between legal immigration and illegal, or undocumented, immigration. Legal immigration is immigration that is approved by the government, such as through a passport or visa (temporary permission to be in the country). Asylum seekers wanting refugee status also fall under the category of legal immigration, but they do not require paperwork before entering the United States. Rather, they apply for asylum once they have entered the country. Illegal immigration is immigration that occurs outside of government-approved methods. It can involve crossing the border outside a port of entry or, more commonly, remaining in the country after a visa has expired.

More than thirty-five million legal immigrants currently live in the United States. Of those, twenty-one million are naturalized citizens—they have sworn an oath to the United States and have the right to vote in elections, the freedom to travel abroad with a US passport, and other legal rights and protections. Of those eligible to become naturalized citizens, only two-thirds have done so. The others remain unnaturalized for a variety of reasons, including significant barriers (such as the English proficiency test typically required or the fee of several hundred dollars). Some immigrants may also choose to remain residents rather than pursue American citizenship.

To become a citizen, an individual must live in the United States with a green card (as a legal permanent resident) for at least five years. A green card allows an immigrant to work legally, travel abroad, and receive some federal benefits. The Immigration and Nationality Act of 1965 gave greater weight to family-based immigration. So if an immigrant has a family member in the United States who is a citizen or a legal permanent resident, it is easier for them to get a green card. More than 60 percent of green cards granted every year go to people in this group. Because of the annual quota, some people wait in line for years—sometimes more than twenty—to gain entry to the United States by this method. Immediate relatives (spouses, children, and parents) of adult citizens have an easier time getting a green card because there are no quotas for them.

PROFILE: **ELON MUSK**

Elon Musk is an outspoken entrepreneur, founder of PayPal and SpaceX, and CEO of Tesla, the most popular electric vehicle maker in the world. Born in South Africa, he left to seek economic opportunity in the United States. He is one of the world's richest people and advocates both for nonpolluting energy and for space exploration to make humanity a "multi-planetary species."

Critics who wish to reduce immigration sometimes refer to this process of family-based migration as chain migration, as if the family is creating a chain or rope from the United States to their home country, so that other family members can more easily enter. But the family-based system has been one of the country's main drivers of immigration since the 1800s. Many critics may even be products of family-based immigration themselves. It is essentially a system of personal referral.

The benefits are simple: family members of people already in the United States have a more stable support system and a built-in community when they arrive, so they are more likely to find a job and be productive members of society. They are also less likely to rely on government services, experience homelessness, or resort to criminal activity for income.

Green cards are also issued to people who do not have family living in the United States. Refugees receive about 13 percent of available green cards. People coming to the United States for employment and skill-based workers make up 12 percent of green card recipients. About 50,000 individuals (5 percent) are given green cards under the diversity lottery program. This program grants green cards to immigrants from nations with small and underrepresented US populations. Registered applicants are selected at random by lottery. In 2019, more than 11 million people applied for the program, and since 1995, more than 1.2 million people have gained entry to the country this way.

GOVERNMENT OVERSIGHT

The Department of Homeland Security was created in 2002 to prepare for and respond to security threats against the American homeland, such as terrorist attacks. The department consolidated twenty-two federal agencies under its command, including those related to immigration services and enforcement. Currently three agencies oversee immigration:

- US Citizenship and Immigration Services processes and rules on applications for citizenship, permanent residency, refugee status, visas, and asylum.
- US Customs and Border Protection is tasked with protecting the nation's 328 ports of entry from terrorism, human and drug smuggling, illegal immigration, and agricultural pests and diseases, all while assisting legal travel and trade.

- Immigration and Customs Enforcement (ICE) is tasked with identifying, investigating, and dismantling security weaknesses at the border. It is also responsible for enforcing federal immigration laws throughout the United States.

UNDOCUMENTED IMMIGRANTS

Undocumented immigrants are people. It is all too easy to reduce the undocumented to statistics or to dehumanize the whole population through the label of "illegal." Undocumented immigrants are mothers, fathers, grandparents, children, students, friends, neighbors, and coworkers. By choice or not, they entered the United States without following immigration guidelines set by the government. Because they lack an official document proving the government granted them the right to reside in the United States (such as a birth certificate, passport, or visa), they are often called undocumented.

While a common perception is that these immigrants all crossed the nation's borders illegally, many initially arrived legally on temporary visas and then stayed in the United States after their visa deadlines expired. Estimates by the Pew Research Center show that since 2010, a large majority of undocumented immigrants in the United States have overstayed their visas. An estimated ten to eleven million undocumented immigrants (about 3 percent of the total US population) live in the United States, though the number fluctuates year to year. The exact number is difficult to come by because most undocumented immigrants tend to avoid official counts to prevent legal trouble.

Choosing to come to the United States without documentation or to overstay a visa is risky. Why would a person do this? Many undocumented immigrants have determined that a life in the United States, even one with risk, is preferable to a life in their home country. The United States offers more jobs and opportunities than

many other countries. Some undocumented immigrants are fleeing violence or natural disaster. With a limited number of visas granted by the government each year and sometimes a decades-long wait to renew a visa or to get into the United States by legal means, many undocumented immigrants make a tough choice to risk illegal immigration status.

Some undocumented immigrants don't even know about their legal status. Such was the case with Jose Antonio Vargas. When Vargas was sixteen, he attempted to get his driver's permit using his green card as proof of identification. But as Vargas explains, "When I handed the clerk my green card as proof of US residency, she flipped it around,

Journalist Jose Antonio Vargas spoke onstage during "I Am an Immigrant: A Celebration of Our Stories," a live event celebrating immigrant heritage on June 18, 2016.

examining it. 'This is fake,' she whispered. 'Don't come back here again.'" He came to the country from the Philippines as a boy, and his grandparents were already naturalized citizens, so he was confused about the situation. His mom sent him to the United States, and his grandparents purchased fake documents without ever informing him of his status. This is an all-too-common situation for immigrants brought to the country as children. Lawyers told Vargas he should lay low and hope for the immigration laws to change, but he was determined to change attitudes about the undocumented. At great risk to himself, he decided to write about his experience in a 2011 *New York Times* article. Vargas has gone on to become an activist and Pulitzer Prize–winning journalist with the *Washington Post*.

WHERE ARE UNDOCUMENTED IMMIGRANTS FROM?

Undocumented immigrants come to the United States from everywhere in the world, just as legal immigrants do, but Mexicans make up the largest group, with a population of about five million. Mexican immigrants make up about 47 percent of the total undocumented population.

The next largest group of undocumented immigrants, about 1.9 million people, comes from Central America—mainly El Salvador, Guatemala, and Honduras. This trio of countries is sometimes called the Northern Triangle because these countries form a triangle in the northern region of Central America. Many people leave this region due to increasing environmental challenges related to climate change, a lack of economic opportunity, and violence caused by political instability.

The third-largest undocumented immigrant population, about 1.5 million people, comes from Asia, especially China and India, the most populous countries in the world. Many come to reunite with family members already in the United States, while others come to find better job opportunities.

HOW DO WE ESTIMATE THE NUMBER OF UNDOCUMENTED IMMIGRANTS?

Since some undocumented immigrants avoid being included in official government records, a frequently used method to determine their numbers is to examine census data to determine the total foreign-born population and then to deduct lawful immigrants from that number. The remainder is the estimated undocumented immigrant population.

LATIN AMERICAN FOCUS

In the twenty-first century, waves of immigrants from Central America have arrived at the southern US border to escape violence and destruction in their homelands. Most of this turmoil stems from violence associated with the illicit drug trade. Drug cartels frequently use murder and intimidation to protect their illegal businesses. They threaten politicians, police, journalists, and ordinary citizens who try to expose or interfere with their criminal behavior. They also carry out bloody battles with one another. Most of the drugs produced in Central America find their way to the United States, which is the number one consumer of illegal drugs in the world.

The drug trade has plunged many parts of Mexico, Central America, and South America into a humanitarian crisis. The violence has forced millions to flee north to seek safety. Many of them, including children, walk thousands of miles to the US border, where they seek asylum. They are placed in detention centers while they await approval or rejection of their asylum applications.

Some are able to bypass the immigration system at the border. They make their way across treacherous desert terrain in the

Southwestern United States, hoping to evade Border Patrol agents. When they reach the United States, they live in the shadows, hoping to avoid ICE and other authorities. They might use false Social Security numbers, fake IDs, and other falsified documents to gain employment and government services.

WHERE DO UNDOCUMENTED IMMIGRANTS LIVE?

Undocumented immigrants live in every major US city, and they are quite likely among your neighbors. Around two-thirds of all undocumented immigrants live in six states: California, Texas, Florida, New York, New Jersey, and Illinois. The metropolitan areas with the largest population of undocumented immigrants are New York City, Los Angeles, and Houston. An estimated eight million of the roughly twelve million undocumented immigrants in the United States are working or seeking employment. They make up 5 percent of the nation's workforce, and they tend to concentrate in certain occupations, such as farming, construction, and the service industry.

Undocumented immigrants come from all types of backgrounds. They work to have a roof over their heads, pay the bills, put food on the table, and care for their families. About five million children in the United States have undocumented parents. While most of these kids were born in the United States, approximately seven hundred thousand were not. About 7 percent of the country's K–12 students have at least one undocumented parent.

While many immigrants without documentation worry about deportation, around 1.5 million undocumented immigrants cannot be deported because they have permission to stay in the United States. Either they have applied for asylum and have pending cases or they have been granted temporary protected status and are able to work legally. The majority of these immigrants are from El

Salvador and Honduras, where the illicit drug trade has caused widespread violence, and Haiti, where natural disasters and political instability have led to a struggle for survival. Undocumented immigrants who came to the United States as children can receive protection from deportation through DACA (Deferred Action for Childhood Arrivals).

SANCTUARY CITIES

ICE is the main federal agency responsible for deporting undocumented immigrants. Because ICE has a small number of agents compared to the undocumented population, the agency often relies on local law enforcement to identify and arrest undocumented individuals.

The level of cooperation between local police departments and federal immigration officials is different from state to state and city to city. States do not have the authority to either deport or legalize undocumented immigrants, but they can set their own laws on issues related to undocumented immigrants. For example, some states check the immigration status of someone applying for a driver's license while others do not.

Some local and state governments are aggressive about apprehending undocumented immigrants. Others are less strict and choose to not allocate resources to pursuing the undocumented. Cities, counties, and states that don't cooperate fully with the federal government's attempts to locate, detain, and deport undocumented immigrants are called sanctuary cities.

The issue of sanctuary cities has become politically charged. Some believe that sanctuary cities encourage further illegal immigration. Others take their criticism further. In late 2022, Florida governor Ron DeSantis and Texas governor Greg Abbott went as far as flying immigrants from Texas to sanctuary cities around the country. Former US attorney general Jeff Sessions said, "So-called 'sanctuary' policies make all of us less safe because they intentionally undermine our laws and protect illegal aliens who have committed crimes." The idea that foreign criminals are roaming free in sanctuary cities is a common complaint. Politicians have attempted to defund, or cut federal funding for, sanctuary cities and states, but federal courts have rejected those efforts.

Supporters of sanctuary cities argue that immigration law is federal law and that local police have more pressing priorities. They note that police departments don't enforce other federal laws, such as federal tax laws. They say that police work is about keeping cities safe. In fact, many police departments state that pushback against sanctuary cities can make it harder to keep cities safe because it often makes immigrants feel reluctant to talk to law enforcement officials about what is happening in their communities.

Many police chiefs say that helping the federal government enforce immigration laws makes cities less safe because it makes immigrants fearful, which in turn makes them less likely to talk to police. If police officers are perceived as immigration officials, immigrants might be afraid to report crimes, serve as witnesses, or share details with investigating detectives. Brian Manley, former police chief of Austin, Texas, said, "Criminals understand that, and they will feel emboldened to commit crimes against the immigrant community without fear of being held accountable because they know they won't call police. It creates a haven for crime."

WORKPLACE RAIDS

With or without the help of local officials, ICE enforces immigration policies in a number of ways. Tactics include workplace raids. When ICE suspects that a large number of employees at a business are undocumented, it first collects evidence and then applies for a search warrant from a judge. The search warrant allows ICE to legally raid the workplace. Armed ICE agents encircle the facility and do not allow anyone to leave without permission. They question employees and then arrest and detain those who are unable to prove their legal status.

DACA AND THE DREAMERS

Imagine living your whole life in the United States as just another American kid, a child of immigrants. Then one day you find out from your parents or the government that you are not in the country legally. What a shock that must be! Almost eight hundred thousand US immigrants who were brought to the country as children are registered with the DACA program. In 2012, then secretary of homeland security Janet Napolitano created the program to provide relief from deportation and to allow these immigrants to work. Most of them have only vague memories—or none whatsoever—of their birth countries and have only ever known the United States as their home.

DACA recipients must renew their participation in the program every two years. Under the administration of President Donald Trump, the government briefly stopped the program and announced that it would not accept new applications. After multiple lawsuits, the Supreme Court determined that the Trump administration's attempt to end the program was unlawful. There are currently efforts to provide a pathway to citizenship for those in DACA, a process that would need to be approved by Congress.

Another effort to assist young undocumented immigrants is the Development, Relief, and Education for Alien Minors (DREAM) Act. It was first introduced in Congress in 2001. According to the act, a person could become a resident of the United States for up to ten years if they met the following conditions:

- They entered the United States under the age of eighteen.
- They entered four years prior to the bill's enactment and have been in the United States since.
- They have been admitted to college or technical school, have graduated from high school or obtained a general equivalency diploma (GED), or are currently working toward a high school diploma or GED.
- They have not been convicted of a serious crime or a drug offense.
- They have not been convicted of a crime of domestic violence.

The next step for a DREAMer would be to obtain a green card by meeting one of these requirements:

- They completed at least two years of college or technical school.
- They completed at least two years of military service, with an honorable discharge.
- They have been employed at least 75 percent of the time for three years.

After five years, a DREAMer with lawful permanent residence status could then apply for naturalization and become a US citizen.

Since 2001, at least ten different versions of the act have been considered, though none have become law. Every version of the DREAM Act has been slightly different, but the key goal is to establish a pathway to legal residency for young people brought to the country as children.

In July 2021, a federal judge ruled that DACA was unconstitutional and prevented new applications to the program. But people currently protected by DACA may keep and renew their status. Activists are pushing for Congress to enshrine DACA into law.

Raids tend to make headlines because of their highly visual nature and their effect on the community and local businesses. One famous raid, in 2008, happened at a slaughterhouse called Agriprocessors in Postville, Iowa. In all, ICE arrested about four hundred undocumented employees, the majority of whom were Guatemalan. Most of these people were eventually deported after serving brief prison sentences.

Critics of raids say that they are extremely costly to conduct, create fear, and are destructive to communities. ICE also sometimes mistakenly detains US citizens during raids. Do workplace raids deter

PROFILE: **KAMALA HARRIS**

Kamala Harris is the first woman and woman of color to be vice president of the United States. Prior to holding that office, she was attorney general of California and a US senator from that state. Harris was born in Oakland, California. Her mother was born in India, and her father is from Jamaica. She is an inspiration to children of immigrants and an example of what is possible in America.

further illegal immigration? Many say no, because companies still want cheap labor, and undocumented immigrants still want jobs in the United States. As long as these jobs are available, immigrants will continue to take risks to secure better lives for themselves and their families. For every immigrant who is deported, there are dozens more ready to take a chance on crossing the border illegally and trying to secure the American Dream.

COMPREHENSIVE IMMIGRATION REFORM

Businesses and politicians recognize the need for immigrant labor, especially in the farming, factory, and service industries. But there is broad consensus that parts of the immigration system are broken. For many years, politicians have attempted to change immigration laws. They have called for sweeping policy changes called comprehensive immigration reform. Both Democrats and Republicans recognize a need to alter the system, but the two sides have not been able to negotiate an agreement.

Among the general public, interest in immigration reform rises and falls. As a *USA Today* editorial noted, "Pressures to revisit the issue run in cycles, usually paralleling anxiety about the economy, jobs, and national security. When concern slackens, businesses become reliant on cheap labor, consumers welcome the lower prices for food and services, and enforcement is gradually neglected."

The most significant bipartisan (involving both major political parties) effort at comprehensive immigration reform started in 2006, when two powerful senators attempted to pass a new law. Massachusetts Democratic senator Ted Kennedy (brother of former president John F. Kennedy) and Arizona Republican senator John McCain (the Republican nominee for president in 2008) worked for several years to reach an agreement, but they met with sharp resistance, and the effort ultimately failed.

AREAS OF DEBATE

Critics say that immigration laws are outdated and fail to address the nation's changing needs. What would they like to change? Some point to the annual limit of sixty-five thousand H-1B visas—visas given to highly skilled foreign workers. Many US businesses have trouble finding enough employees with these skill sets inside the United States, so they turn to immigrants to fill those positions. Raising the limit on H-1B visas could help with this job shortage.

Another major issue is asylum. Asylum seekers often have to wait many years for a decision on their asylum claims. Since they are seeking protection from danger, many say it shouldn't be so difficult for them to find that safety in the United States. But others argue that that the nation simply can't accommodate all the people seeking protection from violence around the world.

President Ronald Regan signed the Immigration Reform and Control Act of 1986 in the White House's Roosevelt Room on November 6, 1986. The signing was witnessed by Vice President George Bush and Senator Strom Thurmond.

Some believe that amnesty, or forgiving unlawful entry into the country and the use of falsified documents to gain employment, is the answer. An amnesty policy would give undocumented immigrants permanent residency and sometimes a path to citizenship. The Immigration Reform and Control Act of 1986 did just that. Signed into law by Republican president Ronald Reagan, the act granted amnesty to about three million undocumented immigrants. In the twenty-first century, proponents of amnesty argue that it is the only practical solution for dealing with undocumented immigrants. The alternative, deporting more than ten million people, would harm the US economy and be extremely expensive, not to mention exceedingly difficult to accomplish. But opponents of amnesty contend that it would reward undocumented immigrants for entering or staying in the country illegally and that this would only encourage further undocumented immigration.

CHAPTER 5

BACKLASH: PART II

The history of anti-immigrant views dates back to even before the nation's founding, but those feelings have continued into the modern era. Still, few presidential administrations have had as big an effect on immigration as the Donald Trump administration. The Trump administration's words and rhetoric affected immigrants as much as its policies did.

Famously, in his first speech as a presidential candidate in 2015, Trump stoked economic anxiety and resentment against immigrants and foreign countries: "Our country is in serious trouble," he said. "We don't have victories anymore. . . . When was the last time anybody saw us beating, let's say, China in a trade deal? They kill us." Trump continued, "When did we beat Japan at anything? They send their cars over by the millions, and what do we do?"

He reserved his harshest words for Mexico: "When do we beat Mexico at the border? They're laughing at us, at our stupidity. And now they are beating us economically. They are not our friend, believe me. . . . The US has become a dumping ground for everybody else's problems. . . . When Mexico sends its people, they're not sending their best. . . . They're sending people that have lots of problems, and they're bringing those problems [to] us. They're bringing drugs. They're

bringing crime. They're rapists. And some, I assume, are good people."
He went on to attack additional countries: "It's coming from more than
Mexico. It's coming from all over South and Latin America, and it's
coming probably from the Middle East."

Trump used this type of nationalist language and anti-immigrant
hostility to get media attention and to rally those who shared similar
views. Words similar to these were common in the 1850s, during
the rise of the Know Nothing Party, and the 1880s, the era of the
Chinese Exclusion Act, but it had been a long time since such
xenophobic language had been used by a presidential candidate,
much less the eventual winner of the White House. These early words
were a preview of how Trump viewed foreign countries and how he
would treat immigrants throughout his years as president from 2017
to 2021.

The border wall separating the United States and Mexico at San Diego and Tijuana
extends hundreds of feet into the Pacific Ocean. From Tijuana Beach you can see San
Diego's skyline and Imperial Beach in the distance on the other side of the wall.

PROFILE: BARACK OBAMA AND DONALD TRUMP

What do Barack Obama and Donald Trump have in common? In addition to being former presidents of the United States, they are both the children of immigrants. Obama's father was born in Kenya, and Trump's mother was from Scotland. They both came to the United States to seek opportunities for themselves and their families.

Mary Anne MacLeod Trump (left) and Barack Obama Sr. (*right*), pictured here in a photograph displayed on a family wall in Kenya, both came to the US as immigrants.

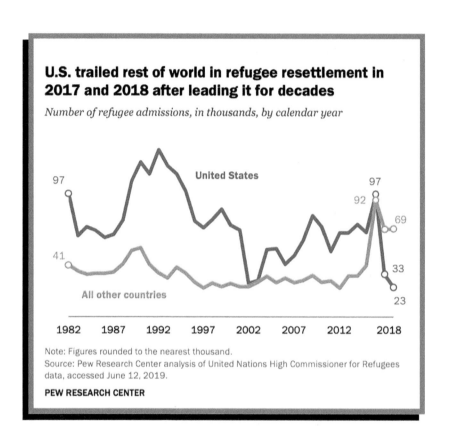

U.S. trailed rest of world in refugee resettlement in 2017 and 2018 after leading it for decades

Number of refugee admissions, in thousands, by calendar year

United States

97

92

97

69

41

33

23

All other countries

1982   1987   1992   1997   2002   2007   2012   2018

Note: Figures rounded to the nearest thousand.
Source: Pew Research Center analysis of United Nations High Commissioner for Refugees data, accessed June 12, 2019.

PEW RESEARCH CENTER

During the Trump Administration, refugee admission to the United States declined considerably. In 2017, Trump initiated a temporary freeze on refugee admissions. By 2019, the Trump administration had only admitted seventy-six thousand refugees in total, nearly 10,000 fewer than the Obama administration admitted in 2016 alone.

THE MUSLIM BAN

On September 11, 2001, Muslim terrorists hijacked US airplanes. They purposely flew two of them into the World Trade Center towers in New York City and one into the Pentagon, a military headquarters near Washington, DC. A fourth plane crashed in rural Pennsylvania after passengers fought back against the hijackers. After these attacks, anti-Muslim hostility soared, as some Americans sought to blame all Muslims for the actions of a small group of radical extremists.

While anti-Muslim sentiments diminished somewhat over time, Trump revived them. During his campaign, he called for a "total and complete shutdown" of Muslim immigration. He got as close as he could to fulfilling that campaign promise by signing an executive order just days into his new administration. This order banned travel for ninety days from seven majority-Muslim countries: Iran, Iraq, Libya, Somalia, Sudan, Syria, and Yemen. It also suspended the resettlement of all Syrian refugees, who were escaping a bloody civil war in their nation.

Trump's order sparked protests across the country and the globe, and lawsuits were filed by US civil rights organizations to block the ban. Trump continued to sign different versions and renewals of the ban. Ultimately, in a 5–4 decision, the Supreme Court voted to uphold the third version of the order. By the end of the Trump presidency thirteen countries had been barred from travel to the United States. President Joe Biden revoked Trump's ban on his first day in office in 2021.

FAMILY SEPARATION

Trump railed against undocumented immigrants in May 2018. "These aren't people. These are animals," he said. His administration declared "zero tolerance" for the undocumented. To deter and discourage immigration, in April 2018 Trump instituted a family separation policy at the southern US border. For several months, immigrants at the border were separated from their families, held in detention facilities, and often deported. In all, 4,368 children, including infants, were stripped from their parents' arms with no plans to reunite them. Fourteen hundred parents were deported without their children. Meanwhile, many of these children were kept in metal cages, a remarkable visual that made headlines across the country. Ultimately, even Trump's closest allies viewed the policy as inhumane and encouraged him to end it. In June 2018, the policy was rescinded, but the damage had been done. Most were reunited, but more than 270 migrant children had yet to be returned to their family at the end of 2021.

By 2021, thousands of children remained separated from their families in detention centers on the US southern border. The pods in the Donna Department of Homeland Security holding facility (*shown above*) housed hundreds of children each in a building only 3,200 sq. feet (297 sq. m) in size.

REMAIN IN MEXICO

The Trump administration's Migrant Protection Protocols, known as the Remain in Mexico policy, implemented in January 2019 forced migrants into tent encampments in Mexico while they awaited a hearing with a US immigration judge. This affected roughly seventy thousand asylum seeking migrants from Central and South America. The conditions in these centers were unsanitary and unsafe, and they made it difficult for immigrants to meet the attorneys representing their asylum cases. In 2021, a federal judge blocked President Biden's attempt to end the initiative. But in the summer of 2022, the Supreme Court sided with the Biden administration and the policy was discontinued.

THE WALL

The political border between the United States and Mexico was established after the Mexican-American War with the signing of the Treaty of Guadalupe Hidalgo in 1848. The border stretches almost 2,000 miles (3,219 km), from the Pacific Ocean to the Gulf of Mexico. Much of this distance is covered by a natural barrier between the two countries, the Rio Grande.

In 1911 a fence was built along the border between California and Mexico to prevent cattle from crossing from one country to the other. Also in the early 1900s, both countries built fences to manage immigration and trade. As anti-immigrant sentiment increased in the 1930s and 1940s, the United States built more physical barriers to keep people of Mexican descent from entering the country. Many migrants found ways around these barriers. This often meant crossing difficult or dangerous landscapes, such as scorching hot deserts.

The construction of border fences increased in the 1990s and the first decade of the 2000s. Under President Bill Clinton, the United States constructed a 14-mile (23 km) wall along the Mexican border between the community of Otay Mesa and the city of San Diego in California. As anti-immigration sentiments continued in the early 2000s, President George W. Bush passed the Secure Fence Act of 2006. This authorized the funding of 700 miles (1,127 km) of additional fencing along the southern border. Bush said that the act was intended to "make [US] borders more secure." But although fences have been shown to decrease unauthorized border crossings at specific points, experts have argued that they merely force determined migrants to cross in other areas.

Perhaps nothing epitomized the immigration policies of Donald Trump more than his call for a physical wall along the full Mexican-US border. During the campaign and throughout his presidency, Trump said he would stop illegal immigration and called for building a wall, which he promised Mexico would pay for. Trump called for a larger

wall that would stretch the length of the border, but both Mexico and the US Congress were unwilling to pay for it.

Critics said that a wall would be extremely expensive to build and would be ineffective at keeping people out, noting that almost all walls can be climbed and scaled. To build a full wall, the government would have had to purchase privately owned land, which would have been extremely expensive as well as time-consuming. Critics also said that a wall would cause damage to the environment by restricting the natural flow of water and animals. When it rains, water that does not soak into the ground needs to flow to rivers and other bodies of water. A wall would block this flow and create pools of standing water. Also, animals do not recognize borders. They are accustomed to roaming freely to mate, find food, and migrate during different seasons. A wall would interfere with these natural processes, leading to declining

In 2017, the Trump Administration signed Executive Order 13767, ordering the Federal Government to direct federal funding toward a wall along the southern border. However, construction was halted in 2018 due to a partial government shutdown.

animal populations. Further, existing border walls are already equipped with motion detectors, underground sensors, and video cameras to help Border Patrol agents apprehend illegal crossers. Some suggested that instead of building a physical wall as Trump desired, the United States should simply use more of this technology, which is less damaging to the environment and is cheaper.

Trump persisted in his quest for a wall and secured $3.6 billion by using money previously allocated for national emergencies. By the end of 2020, 423 miles (681 km) of new fencing and barriers had been built, but US Customs and Border Protection confirmed that almost all of this construction was a replacement for old or deteriorating existing barriers. Biden, once in office, paused the construction of additional barriers but did approve closing gaps in the existing wall along the Arizona border in 2022.

COVID-19

Starting in late 2019, the disease COVID-19 began to spread around the globe. As countries around the world tried to slow its spread, the Trump administration seized the opportunity to attack immigrants once more. Citing the pandemic, Trump closed the southern border by forcing the Center for Disease Control (CDC) to invoke Title 42. This law allows the government to shut down borders to prevent the spread of disease. It overrides normal protections and procedures for immigrants at the border, including unaccompanied minors and asylum seekers. It allows the government to immediately expel would-be immigrants rather than holding them in detention centers or processing centers. The CDC initially refused to issue the emergency rule, as "there was no valid public health reason," but the agency eventually bowed to White House pressure. Critics of the move noted that businesspeople, tourists, and legal immigrants were still allowed to cross the border, so the move was clearly designed to keep undocumented immigrants out rather than to protect public health.

The COVID-19 Hate Crimes Act was passed in 2021 as a response to the rise in anti-Asian violence. Representative Judy Chu spoke about the bill and the effect of hate crimes on the Asian American community.

Anti-immigrant forces took advantage of the COVID-19 pandemic in other ways. The virus had emerged in Wuhan, China, so some Americans blamed China for the pandemic. In the United States, hostility against all people of Asian descent—whether they traced their heritage to China or another Asian nation—began to soar. In 2020, hate crimes against Asian Americans rose 149 percent. In Cleveland, Ohio, Thai American Kiwi Wongpeng was stopped at a traffic light when a man pulled up next to her and shouted, "Get out of my country—that's an order! I'll kill you."

Such hatred and hostility was stoked by Trump, who frequently called COVID-19 the "China virus" and the "Kung-flu," insensitive terms that laid the blame for the virus on all people of Asian descent. Others called Asian Americans diseased, an old insult thrown at immigrants more than 150 years ago.

CHAPTER 6

DEBUNKING MYTHS ABOUT IMMIGRANTS

Immigration is an issue that stirs emotions and political passions. Some choose to see themselves or their family histories in immigrants—another generation of newcomers pursuing the American dream. Others may see immigrants as outsiders and the cause of societal changes. As we've seen throughout history, when people do not have accurate information and facts, it is much easier for rumors, misconceptions, and misinformation to fill the void. Because immigration involves real human beings, it is important to dispel the myths that have developed around immigration. Misinformation can easily lead to suspicion and prejudice, which can be manipulated to encourage people to violence. Examples of this are the hate crimes against the Asian community in response to the COVID-19 pandemic or the January 6, 2021, attack on the US Capitol. By examining the truth or inaccuracy of these myths, we can better inform ourselves about what immigration is, what it isn't, and what we should do about it.

MYTH 1: IMMIGRANTS DON'T LEARN ENGLISH.

TRUTH: IMMIGRANTS DO LEARN ENGLISH; SOME MORE QUICKLY THAN OTHERS.

The idea that immigrants don't learn English has been a common critique since Benjamin Franklin complained about German immigrants in the 1750s. There have even been nativist movements to make English the official language of the country, although such efforts have not led to any policy changes. As the world becomes more interconnected, many people argue that making America "English

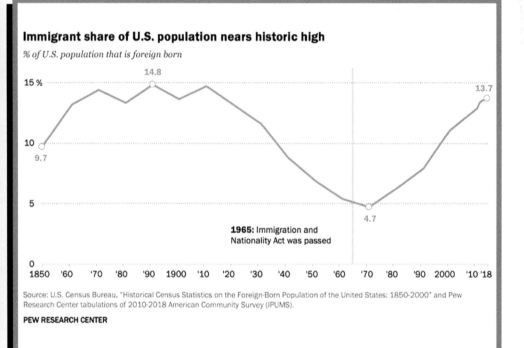

Immigrant share of U.S. population nears historic high

% of U.S. population that is foreign born

14.8

13.7

9.7

4.7

1965: Immigration and Nationality Act was passed

1850 '60 '70 '80 '90 1900 '10 '20 '30 '40 '50 '60 '70 '80 '90 2000 '10 '18

Source: U.S. Census Bureau, "Historical Census Statistics on the Foreign-Born Population of the United States: 1850-2000" and Pew Research Center tabulations of 2010-2018 American Community Survey (IPUMS).

PEW RESEARCH CENTER

According to several years of census data from 1980 to 2018, consistently over 45 percent of foreign-born Americans are proficient in English.

only" would drive away tourism, hurt immigrant communities, and negatively affect the economy.

When non-English–speaking immigrants come to the US, they often lean on others to help them understand what English speakers are saying, but the majority do eventually learn at least conversational English. According to a 2012 study, immigrants are learning English faster than previous generations and 66 percent of immigrants who speak a foreign language at home can speak English "very well" or "well." In many parts of the country, the demand for English-as-a-second-language classes are outpacing their availability. This shows an eagerness among non-English–speaking immigrants to learn the language.

But the most significant factor that determines whether an immigrant is able to learn English is age. Young people, in general, learn new languages more quickly than older adults. When it comes to the children of immigrants, nearly all of them speak fluent English because they have grown up surrounded by it in school, media, and entertainment.

MYTH 2: IMMIGRANTS STEAL JOBS FROM CITIZENS.

TRUTH: IMMIGRANTS DO JOBS MANY CITIZENS ARE UNWILLING OR, IN SOME CASES, UNQUALIFIED TO DO.

This complex issue has been a driver of anti-immigrant sentiment since the early waves of the 1800s. Despite the hostility immigrants sometimes face, they find work in the United States because there is a demand for it. Many industries throughout history would not have existed or succeeded without immigrant labor. Such industries include the early railroads, factories, construction, agriculture, domestic services, and more.

Immigrant workers usually do not compete with American workers as much as they tend to compete with other immigrants. The oft-used phrase is that "immigrants do the jobs citizens won't do." Undocumented immigrants often fill jobs for which there are simply not enough available workers in the US. For example, in construction, the demand for home building has recently outpaced the number of people working in construction. This causes companies to seek labor from outside the United States. This is also true in farming and agriculture. Immigrants have historically filled that void, and they continue to do so.

Further, workers to fill low-skilled jobs are not the only employees in demand. Many companies in technology and engineering industries say they can't find enough citizens who are qualified for some highly skilled jobs. These companies have turned primarily to Indian and Chinese immigrants, whose home countries emphasize math and science, to fill the demand. Companies often sponsor their entry into the country by applying for special green cards. Although there are limits on these high-skilled worker visas, many companies are pushing the government to raise the per-country limit to meet this demand.

MYTH 3: IMMIGRANTS DON'T PAY TAXES.

TRUTH: LEGAL AND UNDOCUMENTED IMMIGRANTS PAY TAXES.

Anyone living and working in the United States pays taxes. A sales tax is added on purchases of many goods, and because immigrants buy goods, they pay this tax. Even apartment renters indirectly pay property taxes because building owners usually factor these taxes into rental rates. Collectively, immigrants earned an estimated $1.5 trillion in total income and paid $405 billion in federal, state, and local taxes in 2017.

Undocumented immigrants also contribute to the nation's Social Security fund, which benefits all citizens. Social Security is a federal program that uses taxes paid into a fund to give benefits to retired or disabled people or survivors who qualify. Although they are not eligible to receive these benefits because undocumented immigrants don't have Social Security numbers (SSN), a large number still pay into the program through the payroll tax. Payroll tax is taken out of most paychecks and is the main source of funds for Social Security. According to estimates, undocumented immigrants added $13 billion to Social Security funds and $3

President Roosevelt signed the Social Security Act on August 14, 1935. This act created the Social Security program and provided insurance against unemployment.

billion to Medicare, a government health insurance program, in 2016 alone. The Social Security Administration's own chief actuary reported three years earlier that undocumented immigrants contributed $12 billion.

When undocumented workers apply for a job, they will often use a fake SSN or someone else's SSN. Some states require employers to check the SSN with a federal database called E-Verify, but most do not. When a worker is paid, the payroll tax is deducted, regardless of citizenship status. Other undocumented workers who are self-employed will often still file taxes with the government using an Individual Taxpayer Identification Number issued by the government. They do this so they will be in good standing with the government if they apply for legal residency someday. This allows them to prove how long they have been in the US and show they are of "good moral character," which can help their case for citizenship.

MYTH 4: IMMIGRANTS ARE A BURDEN ON GOVERNMENT SERVICES AND BENEFITS.

TRUTH: IMMIGRANTS PAY MORE INTO SERVICE AND BENEFITS THAN THEY RECEIVE.

Immigrants mainly come to the United States to work or to reunite with family, not to live off government services. Almost all government assistance programs demand proof of legal immigration status. As of 1996, federal law prohibits immigrants from receiving most benefits until they have been in the country for at least five years. Undocumented immigrants are not eligible to receive public assistance like welfare, food stamps, or Medicaid (government-subsidized health insurance for low-income individuals).

For basic humanitarian reasons, the government does allow undocumented immigrants access to schooling and emergency medical care. As the US Chamber of Commerce says, "Economists view expenditures on health care and education for children as investments that pay off later, when those children become workers and taxpayers." As explained earlier, undocumented immigrants pay taxes and help fund these programs despite the possibility of never being able to use them. A 2018 study concluded that natural-born citizens use 27 percent more benefits compared to eligible immigrants of similar incomes and ages.

MYTH 5: IMMIGRANTS BRING CRIME TO COMMUNITIES.

TRUTH: IMMIGRANTS ARE FAR LESS LIKELY TO COMMIT CRIMES THAN CITIZENS.

This myth has been a rallying cry of anti-immigrant movements since before the first large wave of German and Irish immigrants came to the United States. It has also been perpetuated by politicians. Studies over the past several decades concluded that the rate of crime, especially serious crime, is lower among immigrants than it is for natural-born Americans regardless of immigration status, country of origin, or completed education. Incarceration rates are much lower for immigrants than citizens. There is a negative correlation between immigration and crime rates—as immigration rates go up, crime rates go down. From 1990 to 2013, immigration rates tripled, but violent crime declined 48 percent.

While that is a national statistic, this trend continues locally. Crime rates are lower in states with larger populations of undocumented immigrants than states with smaller undocumented populations. For example, El Paso, Texas, a city with one of the highest shares of immigrants in the country, is consistently named one of the safest cities to live in.

Why do immigrants commit fewer crimes than natural-born Americans? Some experts theorize that because immigrants have

made a dramatic and emotional decision to uproot their lives, they are more cautious about behavior that would put them in jeopardy, such as committing a serious crime. Others theorize that because immigrant communities tend to revitalize lower-income neighborhoods with economic growth, crime rates go down as the poverty rates go down.

MYTH 6: TERRORISTS INFILTRATE THE COUNTRY BY CROSSING THE SOUTHERN BORDER.

TRUTH: TERRORISTS GENERALLY DO NOT ENTER THE COUNTRY THROUGH MEXICO.

After September 11, 2001, when terrorists attacked the US, Congress passed the Patriot Act. Although it was not an immigration law, in an effort to secure the nation, the Department of Homeland Security was given authority to track down undocumented immigrants with terrorist ties, check the criminal history of visa applicants, and hold those accused of having terrorist ties indefinitely with no access to an attorney. Despite the fact that most of the 9/11 hijackers were in the country on legal visas and did not cross the southern border, the myth that violent terrorists cross the southern border has persisted. The Department of Homeland Security has recently noted that this belief is unsupported by credible intelligence or facts on the ground. The US Department of State's Bureau of Counterterrorism also reported that there is "no evidence that any terrorist group has targeted U.S. citizens in Mexican territory, and no credible information that any member of a terrorist group has traveled through Mexico to gain access to the United States."

In recent years, top law enforcement officials have noted that the United States' current biggest terrorism threat is domestic terrorism, or attacks committed by US citizens on American soil. In a Senate

Judiciary Committee hearing in 2021, the FBI director warned that agents had opened two thousand domestic terrorism inquiries in recent years. He said that the problem of racially motivated extremists was "metastasizing across the country," and that the number of white supremacists arrested in the United States in 2020 had tripled from three years earlier.

Border Patrol agents apprehend migrants who have crossed the US-Mexico border without legal documentation. These people are often placed in crowded detention facilities until their cases are heard in court.

THE PSYCHOLOGY OF IMMIGRATION

Why do so many readily believe myths about immigration? While the words and actions of some opponents of immigration can be called xenophobic, racist, and discriminatory, and can even turn into hate crimes, not all opponents of immigration fit into these categories. Not all people who oppose immigration are bigots or racists. Some have legitimate concerns about immigration, especially illegal immigration, and its effects on the country. These people argue that the nation has a right to control its border and that the United States is a nation of laws. They argue that if immigration laws are allowed to be broken, then other laws might be broken as well. These are sensible concerns, and this is why immigration is such a complex issue.

Many people have displayed anti-immigrant hostility. Are all of these people bad? Or is there something deeper? Immigration is a deeply emotional issue, and some psychologists believe anti-immigration movements can be examined through the lens of metathesiophobia, or fear of change. Change can be frightening and can cause anxiety. When people see their community and reality changing, the natural instinct for some is to oppose that change. But the reality is, the United States has always been changing and will continue changing as new people, cultures, religions, languages, and identities are brought together. Such is the history of all countries, and as we become more interconnected through social media discomfort with change will likely increase for some.

Psychology also teaches us that it is a built-in tendency to be distrustful of the "other," or the "them" as opposed to the "us." It is widely believed that in prehistoric times, this suspicion of others helped keep us alive. In the modern era, this instinct can push us into bigotry and discrimination. Human psychology and our natural instincts are extremely influential over the actions of people. If we see a puppy, we want to pet it, and when a stranger walks toward us on a dark street, we often want to flee or fight them. When an immigrant comes to town, we may feel that same reaction, especially if they look different from us. Unless we are careful, our brains are often quick to label these people as "outsiders."

When we fear outsiders, our brains often exaggerate their threat. One study by two New York University psychologists in 2012 showed how our brains can do this. In their experiment, people who expressed negative feelings about Mexican immigrants believed Mexico City to be many hundreds of miles closer to New York than people who didn't harbor those same negative feelings. Interestingly, newer studies showed that if people believed there was a secure border wall, the exaggerated threat effect disappeared.

Because our brains are hardwired to be on the lookout for threats to our survival, stories and anecdotes about immigrants can be very powerful, whether they're true or not. As Mina Cikara, a Harvard psychologist, explains, "Once you can get that one story out there, it's enough to start the cycle of people thinking this way and changing how people think about these out-groups. People are very sensitive to anecdotes, more than they are to abstract representations of data." Stories and "things you've heard from someone" can be more powerful because they activate our emotions much more easily than data and facts.

The persuasiveness of fear and emotion in human psychology has been exploited by people, especially politicians, for a long time. If a politician can point to an outsider and say "this person is the problem," they can more easily control people's emotions and influence their decisions and voting habits. Some politicians understand this, and they use this psychological effect to consolidate power, usually for their own personal gain.

Fear is a powerful emotion, but people can be taught to transform their fears into more positive emotions. If emotional anecdotes can be used to create fear, then they can also be used to change minds. Called the identifiable victim effect, this method of changing minds uses images and stories of individuals to create empathy.

As you learn more about a person, you're more likely to empathize with them rather than viewing them as a threat. This was recently seen in America's legalization of gay marriage. In many states, people who changed their attitudes about gay marriage attributed their changed minds to learning that someone they already knew was gay, or to conversations they had with neighbors who knocked on their doors to talk about the issue. This suggests that the more we get to know others, the more we may learn to accept and understand one another.

CHAPTER 7

THE POWER OF A DIVERSE NATION

The United States has benefited enormously from immigration. It has been called a shining city on a hill, a beacon of hope, and a melting pot, and each generation of immigrants that come to its shores helps keep the country vibrant, innovative, and strong. This nation would not be what it is without immigrants, and that's why they are often called "the hands that built America."

As author and historian Chuck Wills said,

> A very incomplete inventory of those building hands would include the Irish and Chinese who laid the railroad tracks that knitted the country together . . . the Poles and Finns and Welsh who forged the steel to make those rails, and who mined the coal to power the trains that ran along them . . . the Germans and Scandinavians and Russians who raised the wheat and meat to feed those miners and factory workers, and who turned the western Plains into the world's breadbasket . . . the African slaves and their descendants who cropped cotton in the scorching fields of the South . . . the French-Canadians and

Armenians who spun that cotton into thread in the mills of New England . . . and the Jews and Italians and Puerto Ricans who wove that thread into clothing in the sweltering sweatshops of New York City.

The American economy has been strong since the beginning of its industrialization in the 1800s when machine-assisted labor replaced manual labor. America became a global powerhouse in 1916, when US output outpaced the entire British Empire for the first time in history. Immigrants helped fuel this explosion in growth as continuous waves of migration provided both cheap and plentiful labor, though this labor was often exploited through US history. Economists and researchers broadly agree that immigration raises total economic output. Immigration increases the number of workers in the labor force, which enhances the economy's ability to produce. Estimates are that immigrants contribute about $2 trillion, about 10 percent of annual gross domestic product. (GDP is the value of all goods and services bought by the final user and produced by the country.) Removal of undocumented immigrants would reduce the GDP by an estimated 2.6 percent.

Perhaps nowhere is the innovative spirit of immigrants more on display than in business. Immigrants are twice as likely as the natural-born population to be small business owners and entrepreneurs. They also founded over 50 percent of the nation's startup companies that are worth over $1 billion, and each of these companies employ an average of 760 people.

Highly skilled immigrants are more likely to have college and advanced degrees and are more likely to work in STEM fields than natural-born Americans are, which leads to a higher rate of innovation. One way to measure innovation is through patents, or inventions. Immigrants generate more patents and are more likely to win Nobel Prizes in physics, chemistry, and medicine. Remember, Nobel Prize–winning physicist Albert Einstein was an immigrant too.

The metaphor of a melting pot was used to promote Israel Zangwill's play of the same name in 1916. The play depicted a Russian Jewish composer who fled to the United States after the 1903 Kishinev pogrom and writes an American symphony. President Theodore Roosevelt attended the opening on October 5, 1908.

Albert Einstein was awarded the Nobel Prize in Physics in 1921 for his discovery of the law of the photoelectric effect. Einstein (*second from the right*) later attended a dinner to honor the 100th year after the birth of Alfred Nobel alongside novelist Sinclair Lewis (*far left*).

DIVERSITY IN CULTURE

The rich diversity of the American population can be seen in its culture. In America a person can find food, music, clothing, and culture from every corner of the globe.

America has a vast and diverse musical landscape. Immigrants and the descendants of enslaved people are responsible for some of the most popular music in the country. Jazz, blues, gospel, Broadway show tunes, Hollywood film scores and, more recently, Latin music fill our ears with sounds that provide the soundtracks to so many lives.

Food options are plentiful, diverse, and delicious. Meals and dishes from other countries have sometimes evolved and become something new, an Americanized hybrid that can even occasionally make their way back to the old country and become popular there too.

In the late 1800s, southern Italians came to America and created a hybrid cuisine rich in garlic and tomatoes. Native Italians mocked it, but it caught on in the US. Italian American dishes, such as spaghetti and meatballs, are some of the most popular in the country. Italian immigrants also brought their winemaking skills, laying the foundation for California's wine industry. Jews from Eastern Europe also brought their food traditions, selling pastrami, knishes, and bagels in delicatessens. Chinese immigrants building the railroads in the 1860s altered their traditional noodle dishes to create chow mein. Chinese American cuisine is the most popular takeout food in the US.

Irish immigrants popularized corned beef and cabbage in America. Mexican food is one of the most popular cuisines in America, and the Tex-Mex hybrid cuisine is responsible for some now-common American foods, such as nachos and fajitas. Salsa is the number one–selling condiment in the country, dethroning ketchup over a decade ago. The history of immigration can be seen in restaurants and popular food options across the United States.

NEXT GENERATION

As populations stagnate and shrink across the globe, the United States' population continues to grow. For example, Japan, facing a

PROFILE: YO-YO MA

If you've heard the beautiful tones of a cello, chances are you've heard them coming from cellist Yo-Yo Ma. Born in Paris to Chinese parents, Ma came to the US as a child to continue his musical studies. Known for crossing genres and cultures, he has introduced his instrument and classical music to a global audience. He has won over fifteen Grammy Awards, and he continues to push musical boundaries. In 2011, President Barack Obama awarded the Presidential Medal of Freedom to Yo-Yo Ma in recognition of the international impact of his music.

shrinking and aging population, recently decided to loosen its strict immigration laws. Although birth rates among US-born citizens have recently started to dip, immigrants have helped keep the overall birth rate steady. Their children are part of our immigrant heritage and are often known as second-generation immigrants. They learn English from youth just like other American citizens, and they assimilate, or integrate. That does not mean they forget their heritage. Many may still honor and respect their ancestral countries or cultures by using and learning their parents' native languages. They may also fly that country's flag and celebrate the holidays and traditions that have helped shape who they are. Subsequent generations may continue these traditions, while also being proud Americans. This is the beauty of America.

WHAT CAN YOU DO NOW?

Are you a first-generation immigrant or perhaps an eighth-generation immigrant? Maybe you're not sure. Most people in the United States trace their roots to immigrants who made the journey here. It can be exciting to find out when your family first came to the US because it can feel a little bit like time traveling.

You can become an amateur genealogist! Genealogy is the study of tracing lines of descent from ancestors. The first step to discovering more about your ancestors is to converse with your relatives. Ask about who they were, where they came from, and what happened to them. Find out if they know birth dates and birthplaces, educations, occupations, and burial locations. Write down what you learn, and record audio of the conversations. This will help you make sure you didn't miss something, and it'll be a nice memento later in life. Ask a parent or guardian about storing this information in an online database. Ancestry.com is a popular site for this. You can even start making a family tree, a visual representation of your line of ancestry.

Check your local library or archives. Librarians and archivists will help in your hunt. Don't forget to search online for sites, such as FamilySearch.org, Ancestry.com, and Archives.com, all of which have a wealth of information. You may find information about border crossings, passports, citizenship and naturalization records, crew lists, passenger lists, and pictures of ancestors you did not know you had.

If you are adopted, some states allow you access to adoption records. Try contacting SearchAngels.org, an organization that specializes in helping people search for their biological families.

Now that you know more about the history of immigration

in the United States, you will likely continue to or begin to notice immigration in the news. When you're eighteen, you can vote for candidates whose views align with how you feel about immigration, but you don't have to wait that long. There are national organizations that you can get involved with right now, such as the National Immigration Law Center, the National Immigration Forum, or the Immigration Advocates Network. You can also search online for immigration organizations in your community. Consider volunteering or working for one. And you can always welcome new people to your community. Getting to know one another's stories is not just a way to make someone feel welcome. It can unite us and make us feel like true neighbors.

Remember that while immigration is an issue that may divide some people, it is what binds us together as a country. There will always be people seeking a better life within its borders and wanting to contribute to the success of the nation. Knowing where we came from and where our neighbors came from can unite us and help us not be afraid of one another. As you learn about your own American story, think about the stories of your friends, your neighbors, and the people in your community whom you don't know. How can you lay out the welcome mat for them?

GLOSSARY

anti-immigration: hostile to or prejudiced against immigrants

anti-Muslim: hostile to or prejudiced against Muslims; related to Islamophobia, a hostility to or prejudice against Muslims, both within and outside a country's borders. Muslims are followers of Islam, a religion founded in the seventh century CE by the prophet Muhammad.

anti-Semitic: hostile to or prejudiced against Jews

asylum seeker: someone who seeks refuge in a foreign country to escape homeland danger and prosecution

bipartisan: marked by or involving cooperation, agreement, and compromise between two major political parties, such as the Democratic and Republican Parties

civil rights movement: a social movement of the 1950s and 1960s that fought to gain equal rights for Black Americans

deportation: the removal of a person from a country

hate crime: a criminal offense motivated by bias or hatred against a member of a group based on that person's race, religion, disability, sexual orientation, ethnicity, gender, or gender identity

incarceration: being imprisoned or confined in a jail

nationalism: a political ideology and movement with the premise that one's own country is inherently superior to all others

naturalized citizen: a person who comes to the United States from a foreign country, fulfills all the legal requirements for citizenship, and takes an oath of loyalty to the country. Naturalized citizens have the same rights and privileges as those born in the country, except the right to be president or vice president.

racism: prejudice, discrimination, or hatred directed at another race, based on the belief that one's own race is superior to all others

refugee: a person who crosses international boundaries to escape homeland violence, civil war, or persecution

sanctuary city: a city with formal and informal policies to help migrants. This may include limiting cooperation with federal immigration enforcement.

temporary protected status: a legal designation that allows eligible people already in the United States to remain in the country for a limited time due to a natural disaster or political strife in their home country

white supremacy: a political ideology and movement that believes that white people are superior to all other races and ethnicities

xenophobia: hostility, fear, or prejudice against people from other countries

SOURCE NOTES

10 "No taxation without representation.": Willard M. Wallace, "American Revolution," *Encyclopedia Britannica*, accessed January 23, 2021, https://www.britannica.com/video/195079/Overview -American-Revolutionary-War.

12 "WHEN in the . . . Pursuit of Happiness.": Willard M. Wallace, "American Revolution," *Encyclopedia Britannica*, accessed January 23, 2021, https://www.britannica.com/topic/Declaration-of -Independence/Text-of-the-Declaration-of-Independence.

16 "What then is . . . rank he holds.": J. Hector St. John de Crèvecœur, "Letters from an American Farmer," available online at the University of Virginia, October 1995, http://Xroads.virginia .edu/~Hyper/CREV/letter03.html.

16 "Here individuals of . . . changes in the world.": Linda Barrett Osborne, *This Land Is Our Land* (New York: Abrams Books for Young Readers, 2016), 9.

19 "produces so richly . . . herbs in blossom.": Gjert Hovland, Dorothy Hoobler, and Thomas Hoobler, *The Scandinavian American Family Album* (New York: Oxford University Press, 1997), 45.

20 "Give me your . . . the golden door!": Emma Lazarus, "The New Colossus," available online at the National Park Service, accessed January 9, 2021, https://www.nps.gov/stli/learn/historyculture /colossus.htm.

37 "We didn't cross the border. The border crossed us.": Nichole Margarita Garcia, "'We Didn't Cross the Border, the Border Crossed Us:' The Importance of Ethnic Studies," *Diverse: Issues in Higher Education*, July 16, 2019, https://www.diverseeducation .com/opinion/article/15104989/we-didnt-cross-the-border-the -border-crossed-us-the-importance-of-ethnic-studies.

38 "If the American . . . for to establish.": Graham Meyer, "Top 40 Chicago Words—Our Contributions to the English Language," *Chicago*, June 23, 2010, https://www.chicagomag.com/Chicago -Magazine/July-2010/Top-40-Chicago-Words-Our-Contributions -to-the-English-Language/.

38 "fashion and home magazines . . . dream and hope.": David Graham Phillips, *Susan Lenox: Her Fall and Rise*, chapter 23, available online at Literature Network, accessed August 18, 2022, http://www.online-literature.com/david-phillips/susan-lenox/23/.

38 "American dream of . . . an independent nation.": James Truslow Adams, *The Epic of America* (Boston: Little, Brown, 1931), available online at Internet Archive, accessed August 18, 2022, https://archive.org/details/in.ernet.dli.2015.262385/page/n7/mode/2up.

43 "to harness the . . . the service of mankind.": Inez Whitaker Hunt, "Nikola Tesla," *Encyclopedia Britannica*, accessed January 4, 2021, https://www.britannica.com/biography/Nikola-Tesla.

45 "The bosom of . . . to it altogether.": Linda Barrett Osborne, *This Land Is Our Land* (New York: Abrams Books for Young Readers, 2016), 9.

45 "Except of useful . . . no use of encouragement": 5.

46 "Why should the . . . Language or Customs.": 6.

47 "any Alien being . . . of good character . . .": 41.

48 "menace . . . peril from Chinese labor": 48.

50–51 "increase of Roman Catholic . . . the American people.": Mae M. Ngai and Jon Gjerde, *Major Problems in American Immigration History: Documents and Essays* (Boston, MA: Wadsworth, Cengage Learning, 2013), 119–120.

51 "full-blooded Caucasians . . . culturally less intelligent": Cybelle Fox and Thomas A. Guglielmo, "Defining America's Racial Boundaries: Blacks, Mexicans, and European Immigrants, 1890–1945," *American Journal of Sociology*, September 2012, https://www.jstor.org/stable/10.1086/666383?seq=1.

56 "the ideal of US homogeneity": "The Immigration Act of 1924 (The Johnson-Reed Act)," Office of the Historian, accessed September 2, 2022, https://history.state.gov/milestones/1921-1936/immigration-act.

57 "This system violated . . . were a country.": Lyndon B. Johnson, "Remarks at the Signing of the Immigration Bill, Liberty Island, New York," available online at the American Presidency Project, https://www.presidency.ucsb.edu/documents/remarks-the-signing-the-immigration-bill-liberty-island-new-york.

61 "multi-planetary species": Erik Gregersen, "Elon Musk," *Encyclopedia Britannica*, accessed January 4, 2021, https://www .britannica.com/biography/Elon-Musk.

64 "When I handed . . . back here again.": Jose Antonio Vargas, "My Life as an Undocumented Immigrant," *New York Times*, June 22, 2011, https://www.nytimes.com/2011/06/26/magazine/my-life-as -an-undocumented-immigrant.html.

69 "So-called 'sanctuary' . . . have committed crimes.": Department of Justice Office of Public Affairs, "Attorney General Sessions Announces Immigration Compliance Requirements for Edward Byrne Memorial Justice Assistance Grant Programs," news release no. 17-826, July 25, 2017, https://www.justice.gov/opa/pr/ attorney-general-sessions-announces-immigration-compliance- requirements-edward-byrne-memorial.

69 "Criminals understand that . . . haven for crime.": Alexia Fernandez Campbell, "US Police Chiefs Are Fighting the Crackdown on 'Sanctuary Cities,' " *Vox*, August 18, 2017, https:// www.vox.com/policy-and-politics/2017/8/18/16130954/police -sanctuary-cities.

73 "Pressures to revisit . . . is gradually neglected.": *USA Today* editors, "Latest Immigration 'Crisis' Defies Simplistic Solutions," *USA Today*, April 19, 2007.

76–77 "Our country is . . . the Middle East.": Amber Phillips, "'They're Rapists,'" President Trump's Campaign Launch Speech Two Years Later, Annotated," *Washington Post*, June 16, 2017, https://www .washingtonpost.com/news/the-fix/wp/2017/06/16/theyre-rapists -presidents-trump-campaign-launch-speech-two-years-later -annotated/.

79 "These aren't people. These are animals.": Gregory Korte and Alan Gomez, "Trump Ramps Up Rhetoric on Undocumented Immigrants: 'These Aren't People. These Are Animals,' *USA Today*, updated May 17, 2018, https://www.usatoday.com/story /news/politics/2018/05/16/trump-immigrants-animals-mexico -democrats-sanctuary-cities/617252002/.

81 "make [US] borders more secure": "Fact Sheet: The Secure Fence Act of 2006," White House, accessed August 18, 2022, https:// georgewbush-whitehouse.archives.gov/news/releases/2006/10 /20061026-1.html.

83 "there was no valid public health reason": Jason Dearen and Garance Burke, "Pence Ordered Borders Closed after CDC Experts Refused," *Associated Press*, October 3, 2020, https://www.apnews.com/article/virus-outbreak-pandemics-public-health-health-new-york-health-4ef0c6c5263815a26f8aa17f6ea490ae.

84 "Get out of . . . I'll kill you.": Jaweed Kaleem, Kurtis Lee, and Melissa Etehad, "Anti-Asian Hate Crimes and Harassment Rise to Historic Levels during COVID-19 Pandemic," *Los Angeles Times*, March 5, 2021, https://www.latimes.com/world-nation/story/2021-03-05/anti-asian-crimes-harassment.

92 "Economists view Expenditures . . . workers and taxpayers.": US Chamber of Commerce, *Immigration Myths and Facts*, April 14, 2016, https://www.uschamber.com/assets/archived/images/documents/files/022851_mythsfacts_2016_report_final.pdf.

93 "no evidence that . . . the United States.": *Country Report on Terrorism 2017*, United States Department of State Publication, September 2018, https://www.state.gov/wp-content/uploads/2019/04/crt_2017.pdf.

94 "metastasizing across the country": Adam Goldman, "Domestic Terrorism Threat Is 'Metastasizing' in U.S., F.B.I. Director Says," *New York Times*, March 2, 2021, https://www.nytimes.com/2021/03/02/us/politics/wray-domestic-terrorism-capitol.html.

96 "Once you can . . . representations of data.": Brian Resnick, "7 Lessons from Psychology That Explain the Irrational Fear of Outsiders," *Vox*, January 30, 2017, https://www.vox.com/science-and-health/2017/1/28/14425658/fear-of-refugees-explained.

98–99 "A very incomplete . . . New York City.": Chuck Wills, *Destination America* (New York: DK, 2005), 8.

SELECTED BIBLIOGRAPHY

Adams, James Truslow. *The Epic of America*. Boston: Little, Brown, 1931. Available online at Internet Archive, accessed September 2, 2022. https://archive.org/details/in.ernet.dli.2015.262385/page/n7/mode/2up.

Bahar, Dany. "The road to fix America's broken immigration system begins abroad." Brookings Institution, December 8, 2020. www.brookings.edu/blog/up-front/2020/12/08/the-road-to-fix-americas-broken-immigration-system-begins-abroad/.

Boissoneault, Lorraine. "How the 19th Century Know Nothing Party Reshaped American Politics." *Smithsonian Magazine*, January 26, 2017. https://www.smithsonianmag.com/history/immigrants-conspiracies-and-secret-society-launched-american-nativism-180961915/.

Budiman, Abby. "Key findings about U.S. immigrants." Pew Research Center, August 20, 2020. www.pewresearch.org/fact-tank/2020/08/20/key-findings-about-u-s-immigrants/.

Ewing, Walter, Daniel Martinez, and Ruben Rumbaut, "The Criminalization of Immigration in the United States." American Immigration Council, July 13, 2015. www.americanimmigrationcouncil.org/research/criminalization-immigration-united-states.

"Family separation under the Trump administration - a timeline." Southern Poverty Law Center, June 17, 2020. www.splcenter.org/news/2020/06/17/family-separation-under-trump-administration-timeline.

Frum, David. "The Real Story of How America Became an Economic Superpower." *The Atlantic*, December 24, 2014. www.theatlantic.com/international/archive/2014/12/the-real-story-of-how-america-became-an-economic-superpower/384034/.

Igielnik, Ruth and Jens Manuel Krogstad. "Where refugees to the U.S. come from." Pew Research Center, February 3, 2017. https://www.pewresearch.org/fact-tank/2017/02/03/where-refugees-to-the-u-s-come-from/.

Jiménez, Tomás R. "Immigrants in the United States: How Well Are They Integrating into Society?" Migration Policy Institute, May 2011. http://www.migrationpolicy.org/research/immigrants-united-states-how-well-are-they-integrating-society.

Kerwin, Donald. "From IIRIRA to Trump: Connecting the Dots to Current US Immigration Policy Crisis." Center for Migration Studies, December 2018. cmsny.org/publications/jmhs-iirira-to-trump/.

Korsten, Dan. "Immigrants as Economic Contributors: Immigrant Entrepreneurs." Immigration Forum, July 11, 2018. www.immigrationforum.org/article/immigrants-as-economic-contributors-immigrant-entrepreneurs.

Krogstad, Jens Manuel. "Key facts about refugees to the US." Pew Research Center, October 7, 2019. https://www.pewresearch.org/fact-tank/2019/10/07/key-facts-about-refugees-to-the-u-s/.

Krogstad, Jens Manuel, Jeffrey S. Passel and D'Vera Cohn. "5 facts about illegal immigration in the U.S." Pew Research Center, June 12, 2019. www.pewresearch.org/fact-tank/2019/06/12/5-facts-about-illegal-immigration-in-the-u-s/.

Lee, Erika. *At America's Gates: Chinese Immigration During the Exclusion Era, 1882-1943*. University of North Carolina Press, 2005.

Moua, Chai Charles. *Roars of Traditional Leaders*. Lanham: University Press of America, 2012.

Musolf, Nell. *The Split History of Western Expansion in the United States*. Mankato: Compass Point Books,#2013.

Nowrasteh, Alex and Robert Orr. "Immigration and the Welfare State: Immigrant and Native Use Rates and Benefit Levels for Means-Tested Welfare and Entitlement Programs." Cato Institute, May 10, 2018. https://www.cato.org/immigration-research-policy-brief/immigration-welfare-state-immigrant-native-use-rates-benefit.

Passel, Jeffrey S. and D'Vera Cohn. "Children of unauthorized immigrants represent rising share of K–12 students." Pew Research Center, November 17, 2016. www.pewresearch.org/fact-tank/2016/11/17/children-of-unauthorized-immigrants-represent-rising-share-of-k-12-students/.

Passel, Jeffrey S. and D'Vera Cohn. "U.S. Unauthorized Immigrant Total Dips to Lowest Level in a Decade." Pew Research Center, November 27, 2018. https://www.pewresearch.org/hispanic/2018/11/27/u-s-unauthorized-immigrant-total-dips-to-lowest-level-in-a-decade/.

Porter, Eduardo. "Short of Workers, U.S. Builders and Farmers Crave More Immigrants." *New York Times*, April 3, 2019. www.nytimes.com/2019/04/03/business/economy/immigration-labor-economy.html.

"Refugees, Asylum-seekers and Migrants." Amnesty International, accessed February 14, 2021. www.amnesty.org/en/what-we-do/refugees-asylum -seekers-and-migrants/.

Roberts, Nina. "Undocumented immigrants quietly pay billions into Social Security and receive no benefits." *Marketplace.org*, accessed February 8, 2021. www.marketplace.org/2019/01/28/undocumented-immigrants-quietly-pay -billions-social-security-and-receive-no/.

Staff Fact Sheet. "The Dream Act, DACA, and Other Policies Designed to Protect Dreamers." American Immigration Council, August 27, 2020. www .americanimmigrationcouncil.org/research/dream-act--daca-and-other -policies-designed-protect-dreamers.

Wali, Alaka. "Democracy and the Iroquois Constitution." The Field Museum, April 26, 2021. https://www.fieldmuseum.org/blog/democracy-and-iroquois -constitution.

Wallace, Sandra Neil and Rich Wallace. *First Generation: 36 Trailblazing Immigrants and Refugees Who Make America Great.* New York: Hachette Book Group, 2018.

Zedillo, Ernesto. "Rethinking the 'war on drugs': Insights from the US and Mexico." voxEU.org, April 22, 2016. Voxeu.org/article/rethinking-war-drugs -insights-us-and-mexico.

FURTHER READING

Gardner, Howard. *Changing Minds: The Art and Science of Changing Our Own and Other People's Minds*. Boston: Harvard Business School Press, 2004.

Marsh, Abigail. *The Fear Factor: How One Emotion Connects Altruists, Psychopaths, and Everyone In-Between*. New York: Hachette Book Group, 2017.

Martinez, Pedro Santiago. *Eclipse of Dreams: The Undocumented-Led Struggle for Freedom*. Chico, CA: AK Press, 2020.

McPherson, Stephanie Sammartino. *The Global Refugee Crisis: Fleeing Conflict and Violence*. Minneapolis: Twenty-First Century Books, 2019.

Needleman, Jacob. *The American Soul: Rediscovering the Wisdom of the Founders*. New York: Penguin Putnam, 2002.

Tisch, Andrew, and Mary Skafidas. *Journeys: An American Story; 72 Essays about Immigration and American Greatness*. New York: RosettaBooks, 2018.

Tobar, Hector. *Translation Nation: Defining a New American Identity in the Spanish-Speaking United States*. New York: Riverhead Books, 2005.

INDEX

PHOTO ACKNOWLEDGMENTS

Image credits: Lumiereist/Shutterstock, pp. 4, 8, 22, 44, 58, 76, 86, 98; NordNordWest/ Wikimedia Commons (Public Domain), p. 5; Science History Images/Alamy Stock Photo, p. 6; SAUL LOEB/AFP/Getty Images, p. 7; Anonymous cartographer/Wikimedia Commons (Public Domain), p. 9; Classic Image/Alamy Stock Photo, p. 11; National Archives (1667751), p. 13; Heritage Art/Heritage Images/Getty Images, p. 15; FLHC11/ Alamy Stock Photo, p. 17; Library of Congress, pp. 19, 39, 90; HUM Images/Universal Images Group/Getty Images, p. 20; Published in Harper's Weekly, (New York) November 7, 1874/Wikimedia Commons (Public Domain), p. 24; Science History Images/ Alamy Stock Photo, p. 25; Sharon Mollerus/Wikimedia Commons (CC BY 2.0), p. 26; Detroit Photographic Co./FPG/Hulton Archive/Getty Images, p. 27; Dorothea Lange/ PhotoQuest/Getty Images, p. 29; "Key findings about U.S. immigrants" Pew Research Center, Washington, D.C. (AUGUST 20, 2020), https://www.pewresearch.org/fact-tank/2020/08/20/key-findings-about-u-s-immigrants/, pp. 31, 87; John Phillips/Getty Images for BoF VOICES, p. 33; Tom Williams/CQ Roll Call/Getty Images, p. 34; Frans Schellekens/Redferns/Getty Images, p. 35; National Archives (532858), p. 41; Hulton Archive/Getty Images, p. 42; ullstein bild/ullstein bild/Getty Images, p. 43; Tomasz Skoczen/Getty Images, p. 46; Bachrach/Getty Images, p. 50; National Archives (537044), p. 55; LBJ Library photo by Yoichi Okamoto, p. 57; NASA/Aubrey Gemignani, p. 59; Paul Morris/Bloomberg/Getty Images, p. 61; Vivien Killilea/Getty Images for SOZE, p. 64; KENA BETANCUR/AFP/Getty Images, p. 71; Bastiaan Slabbers/EPA/Bloomberg/ Getty Images, p. 72; National Archives (75855147), p. 75; Photo Beto/Getty Images, p. 77; Richard Corkery/NY Daily News Archive/Getty Images, p. 78 (left); Peter Macdiarmid/ Getty Images, p. 78 (right); "Key facts about refugees to the U.S." Pew Research Center, Washington, D.C. (October 7, 2019), https://www.pewresearch.org/fact-tank/2019/10/07/ key-facts-about-refugees-to-the-u-s/, p. 79; DARIO LOPEZ-MILLS/POOL/AFP/Getty Images, p. 80; PAUL RATJE/AFP/Getty Images, p. 82; Kent Nishimura/Los Angeles Times/Getty Images, p. 84; JUSTIN HAMEL/AFP/Getty Images, p. 94; University of Iowa Libraries Special Collections Department/Wikimedia Commons (Public Domain), p. 100; Keystone/Getty Images, p. 101; Brooks Kraft LLC/Corbis/Getty Images, p. 103.

Cover: Lumiereist/Shutterstock.